P9-DEB-504

CHOCOLATE
GALORE

CHOCOLATE
GALORE

CAROLINE BARTY

spruce

An Hachette Livre UK Company

First published in Great Britain in 2008
by Spruce, a division of
Octopus Publishing Group Ltd
2–4 Heron Quays, London E14 4JP
www.octopusbooks.co.uk

Copyright © Octopus Publishing Group Ltd
2008

Distributed in the United States and Canada
by Hachette Book Group USA
237 Park Avenue
New York
NY 10017

All rights reserved. No part of this work
may be reproduced or utilized in any form
or by any means, electronic or mechanical,
including photocopying, recording or by
any information storage and retrieval
system, without the prior written permission
of the publisher.

ISBN 13: 978-1-84601-149-8
ISBN 10: 1-84601-149-3

Photography: Ian Garlick
Food Styling: Eliza Baird
Page Layout: Balley Design Associates

A CIP catalogue record of this book is
available from the British Library.

Printed and bound in China

10 9 8 7 6 5 4 3 2 1

This book contains the opinions and ideas of
the author. It is intended to provide helpful
and informative material on the subjects
addressed in this book and is sold with the
understanding that the author and publisher
are not engaged in rendering any kind of
personal professional services in this book.
The author and publisher disclaim all
responsibility for any liability, loss or risk,
personal or otherwise, which is incurred as
a consequence, directly or indirectly, of the
use and application of any of the contents
of this book.

CONTENTS

INTRODUCTION

It is the cacao tree, indigenous to the regions of Central and South America, which provides us with the raw material for making chocolate. The cacao seed or bean is roasted, fermented, dried, and ground to leave cacao (or cocoa) powder.

★ ORIGINS ★

It is generally thought that the Mayans, living in the Yucatán and Guatemala in the first millennia AD, were the first people to cultivate and use the cacao tree. However, evidence suggests that the Mayans learnt their knowledge from an earlier Olmec culture, around 1500–400 BC. Mayan traders would have introduced the cacao bean to the Aztecs and it soon became of huge importance in both cultures. Warriors and noblemen were buried with vessels for drinking chocolate and chocolate was offered to the gods as ceremonial gifts.

Christopher Columbus was known to have brought back some cocoa beans to the Spanish court but it wasn't until later when Cortés returned from the New World that the popularity of the cocoa bean really took off. So a commodity was born that generated great power and wealth. The Spanish were credited with giving chocolate its name—an amalgam of the Mayan "chocol," meaning hot, and the Aztec "atl", meaning water.

By the 1600s chocolate was known throughout Europe although it seems to have been its mythical medicinal qualities that first appealed to people. Chocolate does in fact contain a small amount of phenylethylamine, which is a chemical that produces a feeling of a natural 'high'. It was the arrival of sugar from America that really cemented the popularity of chocolate. Drinking sweetened chocolate became a popular pastime although still only for the wealthy.

★ THE CHOCOLATE BAR ★

The idea of mixing cocoa butter, the by-product of making cocoa powder, with the powder itself came about in the early 1800s. A smooth paste, solid when cold, was created that gave us the early form of what we know as the chocolate bar. It was the Swiss who refined the art of chocolate making by inventing the process known as conching. The chocolate is constantly moved at a temperature of between 131–185°F thus exposing it to air, which improves its flavor and extracts more fat from the cocoa. The Swiss also developed the milk chocolate bar by adding dried milk to the chocolate-making process. White chocolate is not strictly chocolate as it does not contain cocoa mass but is a blend of cocoa butter, sugar, and milk solids.

★ LIMITLESS FLAVORS ★

As the flavor of chocolate improved so chefs were inspired to create wonderful confections. Nuts, fruit, and flavorings were added, chocolate was molded into different shapes, and filled with soft fondant or liqueurs. There is always a heated debate as to which country makes the finest chocolates. Belgium, Switzerland, or France all have a good case to put forward but ultimately it comes down to personal tastes. Some diehard chocoholics would not touch a bitter square of bittersweet chocolate yet others see milk chocolate as an inferior product, barely worthy of being called chocolate at all. Whatever your view there is no disputing that chocolate is one of life's great pleasures.

COOKING WITH CHOCOLATE

As with all things, the better the quality the better the taste, and chocolate is no exception.

Nowadays the range of superior-quality chocolate available is enormous. There is absolutely no excuse to buy what they call chocolate-flavor cake covering. Avoid it at all costs. Professional confectioners tend to use couverture chocolate. It has a high cocoa butter content and so melts easily and when set has a pleasing glossy finish. However, it is only available in specialist shops so is not used in any of these recipes.

For the fullest flavor I recommend chocolate with at least 70% cocoa solids but in some recipes its intensity is overpowering and so a chocolate with 50% cocoa solids actually produces a more delicate flavor. If it is not obvious from the front, if you read the list of ingredients on the back of a bar of chocolate it will tell you the amount of cocoa solids present.

You will also find that chocolate with less cocoa solids will melt more easily and will be less likely to "seize". This is when the chocolate overheats and becomes stiff and grainy. It will also seize when any cold moisture comes into contact with it. This is why it is essential to let melted chocolate cool a little before incorporating it with anything else.

★ MELTING CHOCOLATE ★

I have to say I always use a microwave to melt chocolate but you have to bear in mind that microwave power varies greatly. Start off on high power but for 10–20 seconds at a time. This way you won't burn the chocolate and you will soon find how long your own microwave takes to melt the chocolate. In general it takes between 1 and 2 minutes to melt a bowl of chocolate but obviously the larger the quantity the longer it will take.

If you don't have a microwave you will need to fit a mixing bowl or pudding basin over the top of a saucepan with a small quantity of hot water in the bottom. This is then placed over a gentle heat until the chocolate melts. The most important thing is not to let the bowl come into contact with the water. Not only will the chocolate overheat, but the water sputters out from the sides and comes into contact with the chocolate, which then seizes. Some people with Agas swear by melting chocolate in a bowl in the bottom oven and the few times I have tried this it seems to work very well. In some cases you can melt chocolate over a direct heat but only when the chocolate is being melted with another liquid such as cream. Never melt chocolate on its own over a direct heat.

★ TEMPERING CHOCOLATE ★

Tempering is the name given to the process whereby chocolate is melted and worked to produce a chocolate with a glossy, even finish. If you want a professional finish to confectionery, especially when making molded chocolate, you will need to temper the chocolate. However, it is tricky due to the precise temperatures required for heating and cooling and will take a bit of practice. The simplest method is to melt the chocolate then pour two-thirds onto a marble slab. With a palette knife work it backwards and forwards until it is just on the point of setting. Return it to the remaining third and remelt it. It can now be used for molds and decorations.

CHOCOLATE DECORATIONS

You can buy all sorts of chocolate-based decorations in the supermarket these days, but the quality of chocolate varies greatly so have a go at making your own.

★ CHOCOLATE PIPING ★

The quickest and simplest way for fine chocolate piping is to get a greaseproof paper piping bag, fill with a little melted chocolate and snip a tiny bit off the end. Then you can write or drizzle the melted chocolate over the surface. When it is on the point of setting chocolate ganache (see page 154) can be piped using an ordinary piping bag and starred nozzle.

★ GRATING CHOCOLATE ★

The microplane graters do a good job at grating chocolate. Putting the chocolate in the refridgerator for 15 minutes will make it easier to grate. Try not to handle the chocolate as it will melt more quickly. Wrapping the end of the chocolate in foil will prevent the heat from your hands melting the chocolate.

★ QUICK CHOCOLATE CURLS ★

First make sure the chocolate is at room temperature. With a potato peeler, peel off little curls from the edge of the chocolate bar.

★ CHOCOLATE CARAQUE ★

Another name for big chocolate curls. Melt 4–5oz chocolate and pour over a marble slab. Leave it to harden. It needs to be hard but not completely set. At a 45° angle to the surface draw the blade of a small sharp knife across the chocolate, away from the body. Turn the point of the knife a little as if you are about to trace a circle. The chocolate should form long curls. It is crucial to get the correct angle of the blade and also that the chocolate is at the right temperature. Too hot and the curls will collapse and too cold, i.e. set, and the chocolate will form shards rather than curls.

★ CHOCOLATE LEAVES ★

Firstly you will need the leaves of a non-toxic plant. Rose and bay leaves are best as they have well-defined veins. Wash the leaves and let it dry completely. Melt the chocolate and paint the underside of the leaves with chocolate. Let it harden and set, then carefully peel off the leaves.

BUYING & STORING CHOCOLATE

Always check the use by date on chocolate as some shops are less than scrupulous about their stock turnover. Bittersweet chocolate tends to have a longer shelf life than milk chocolate, about one year compared to six months. Always keep chocolate in a cool, dry place. If it is very hot it can be kept in the refrigerator but it can become discolored due to the difference in temperatures. This does not affect its flavor and it can be used in the normal way.

INGREDIENTS

Before cocoa was mixed with sugar to become chocolate it was used predominantly in savory dishes. Most people have heard of turkey mole and chili con carne, two well-known Mexican dishes, where a little chocolate is added to enhance and add a new dimension. Chapter Seven, New Ways with Chocolate, includes these two favorites and re-introduces chocolate and cocoa into a variety of other main course dishes. Here is a list of the most commonly used ingredients when baking sweet dishes using chocolate.

★ BUTTER ★

Try and use the butter that the recipe specifies. The flavor of salted butter can really spoil a dessert or confectionery, as can cheap margarine.

★ UNSWEETENED COCOA ★

Unsweetened cocoa is chocolate liquor that has had most of the cocoa butter removed and is dried into a very fine powder. Whatever you do don't confuse unsweetened cocoa with drinking chocolate. Unsweetened cocoa is unsweetened and should have no other additives. Dutch unsweetened cocoa is the best as it is processed to reduce the acids that occur naturally in chocolate.

★ PLAIN CHOCOLATE ★

Most recipes will specify which bittersweet chocolate to use, usually between 50 and 70% cocoa solids. Taste different brands to find your favorite.

★ COUVERTURE CHOCOLATE ★

Couverture chocolate is what professional chocolatiers use for their work. It has a high cocoa butter content that when melted, produces a runny chocolate that covers in an even, glossy finish.

★ MILK CHOCOLATE ★

There is a huge difference between good and bad milk chocolate. Try and buy one of the expensive brands and you really will notice the difference, both in flavor and texture.

★ WHITE CHOCOLATE ★

As mentioned, white chocolate is not actually chocolate at all as it contains no cocoa solids. Cheap white chocolate can be tricky to melt and can seize very easily if it comes into contact with a liquid or even a utensil with a different temperature. I always warm a metal spoon under hot water for a minute and dry it really well before using it to stir melted white chocolate.

EQUIPMENT

Apart from the obvious cake pans, muffin pans etc. there is not much specialist equipment needed for cooking with chocolate. However, a sugar thermometer is essential for a few of the recipes in the Chocolaterie chapter and is a great help for other recipes. Most good cookshops sell them. Another invaluable item in the kitchen is nonstick baking parchment. Even if you have non-stick bakeware it is best to baseline your pans. If you have a food processor with a balloon whisk and dough hook attachments all the better, but it is not a necessity. To incorporate as much air as possible into your baking it is best to have an electric hand-held whisk.

THE BAKERY

DOUBLE CHOC-CHIP COOKIES

These cookies are the ultimate chocolate experience—double the chocolate, double the taste!

MAKES 14 COOKIES

1½ sticks (12 tablespoons) butter
⅔ cup superfine sugar
1 egg, beaten
1–2 teaspoons vanilla extract
1¾ cups all-purpose flour
1 teaspoon baking powder
2oz good-quality bittersweet chocolate, broken into pieces
2oz good-quality white chocolate, broken into pieces

1. Preheat the oven to 350°F. Lightly grease a baking sheet.

2. Beat together the butter and sugar until pale and fluffy. Beat in the egg and vanilla extract. Sift the flour and baking powder together and beat into the mixture. Add the chocolate and stir until mixed.

3. Place 5–6 rounded tablespoons of the cookie mixture onto the baking sheet at a time, leaving plenty of space between them as the cookies will almost double in size. Bake for 12–15 minutes until golden.

4. Let cool on the baking sheet for 2–3 minutes, then transfer to a wire rack to cool completely. Cookies can be stored in an airtight container for up to 1 week.

CHOCOLATE GRANOLA BARS

These bars are a sort of spongy flapjack. I like to use a nutty granola but you can use your favorite cereal as long as it is the crunchy variety rather than a muesli.

MAKES 10–12 BARS

1 stick (8 tablespoons) sweet butter,
   slightly softened
²⁄₃ cup light brown sugar
1 egg, beaten
1 cup all-purpose flour
2 cups crunchy granola
3¹⁄₂oz bittersweet chocolate
   (70% cocoa solids),
   finely chopped

1. Preheat the oven to 350°F. Baseline a 9in square cake pan with non-stick baking parchment.

2. Beat the butter and sugar until light and fluffy. Beat in the egg. Fold in the flour followed by the granola and chocolate.

3. Spoon into the prepared pan and level out the surface. Bake for 20–25 minutes until firm to the touch. Cool in the tin, then cut into bars.

WHITE CHOCOLATE & BUTTER PECAN COOKIES

These cookies freeze really well so if you make more than you need pop the cookies in a freezer bag and seal. Defrost at room temperature for one hour.

MAKES ABOUT 30 COOKIES

1½ sticks (12 tablespoons) sweet
   butter, slightly softened
1⅔ cups light brown sugar
¾ cup superfine sugar
2 eggs, beaten
2 teaspoons vanilla essence
2 cups all-purpose flour
1 teaspoon baking powder
Pinch of salt
¾ cups white chocolate morsels or
   finely chopped white chocolate
1 cup pecans, finely chopped

1. Preheat the oven to 350°F.

2. Cream the butter and sugars together until light and fluffy. Beat in the eggs and vanilla extract. Stir in the remaining ingredients in order.

3. Take tablespoons of the dough and roll into balls. Place on a non-stick baking sheet about 2–3in apart and press down slightly. Bake in batches for 10–15 minutes until they are turning golden around the edges.

4. Remove from the oven and let harden for a minute or two before placing on a wire rack to cool completely.

CHOCOLATE HAZELNUT & VANILLA WHIRLS

These attractive and flavorsome little cookies are surprisingly simple to make.

MAKES ABOUT 30 COOKIES

1³⁄₄ sticks (14 tablespoons) butter, plus extra for greasing

¹⁄₂ cup confectioner's sugar

1 teaspoon vanilla extract

2 cups all-purpose flour, sifted, plus extra for dusting

2 tablespoons chocolate and hazelnut spread

1 tablespoon unsweetened cocoa powder, sifted

1. Preheat the oven to 350°F. Lightly grease a baking sheet.

2. Beat together the butter and sugar until pale and fluffy. Beat in the vanilla extract. Add the flour and work into the mixture to form a soft dough.

3. Divide the dough into two pieces and work the chocolate and hazelnut spread and cocoa powder into one half.

4. Roll each piece of dough on a lightly floured surface to form two rectangles about 6 x 8cm. If the dough is too soft to roll, chill wrapped in plastic wrap for 10–15 minutes to firm slightly.

5. Place one piece of dough on top of the other and press together lightly. Trim the edges and roll up lengthwise like a jelly roll. Cover and chill for 30 minutes.

6. Cut the dough into ¹⁄₄in slices and space well apart on the baking sheet. Bake for 10–12 minutes until crisp.

7. Let cool for 2–3 minutes on the baking sheet, then transfer to a wire rack to cool completely. Cookies can be stored in an airtight container for up to 1 week.

COCONUT & CHOCOLATE MELTS

These crisp, short cookies are great with ice cream. Roll out the dough in batches as it is quite dry and will crack if you try to roll it out all in one go.

MAKES 20–24 COOKIES

¾ cup all-purpose flour
¼ cup cornstarch
½ cup confectioner's sugar
¼ cup shredded coconut
1 tablespoon unsweetened cocoa powder, sieved
1 stick (8 tablespoons) butter, diced

1. Preheat the oven to 375°F.

2. Mix together the flour, cornstarch, confectioner's sugar, coconut, and cocoa powder. Rub in the butter until you have a fine breadcrumb mixture. With your hands bring the mixture together to form a ball.

3. Divide the dough into two and, on a floured surface, roll out one piece to a thickness of ⅛in.

4. Stamp out with a cookie cutter and place on a nonstick baking sheet. Bake in batches for 6–8 minutes.

5. Let harden for a couple of minutes before cooling on a wire rack.

CHOCOLATE MACAROONS

Rich, chewy, and utterly delicious. If you really want to gild the lily you could sandwich the macaroons with a vanilla buttercream, but I think they are sublime as they are.

MAKES 12–14 MACAROONS

4oz bittersweet chocolate
  (50% cocoa solids),
  broken into pieces
²/₃ cup superfine sugar
1¹/₃ cups ground almonds
1 teaspoon vanilla extract
2 egg whites
Melted white and supersweet
  chocolate, to decorate (optional)

1. Preheat the oven to 360°F. Melt the chocolate over a pan of hot water or in the microwave for 1–2 minutes. Let cool for a minute or two.

2. Stir in the remaining ingredients, then, with an electric whisk, beat for 2 minutes.

3. Line a large flat baking sheet with nonstick baking parchment. Place tablespoons of the mixture about 3in apart and bake for 12–15 minutes. Cool on a wire rack, then decorate by piping with white and bittersweet chocolate, if liked.

CHOCOLATE REBELS

The unsweetened cocoa powder and oats make these cookies really rich and filling. Best served with a pitcher of really cold milk.

MAKES 24 COOKIES

2 cups rolled oats
1½ cups self-rising flour
⅓ cup unsweetened cocoa powder, sifted
1 cup light brown sugar
½ cup superfine sugar
Pinch of salt
1½ sticks (12 tablespoons) sweet butter, melted
1 egg, beaten
4 tablespoons milk
1 teaspoon vanilla extract
Melted bittersweet chocolate, to decorate (optional)

1. Preheat the oven to 350°F.

2. In a large bowl mix together the oats, flour, unsweetened cocoa, sugars, and salt.

3. In another bowl mix together the melted butter, egg, milk, and vanilla extract.

4. Pour the wet ingredients into the dry ones and mix well.

5. Place tablespoons of the cookie mixture at regular intervals, but not too close together, on a nonstick baking sheet and bake in the preheated oven for 12–15 minutes.

6. Turn onto a wire rack to cool completely. If liked, decorate with piped bittersweet chocolate.

CHOCOLATE TIP
To decorate cookies or cakes with piped chocolate, melt some chocolate (see page 12) and spoon into a small piping bag or small freezer bag. If using a plastic bag, push the chocolate into the corner and snip of tip. Gently squeeze out the chocolate.

THUMBPRINT COOKIES

These cookies are light and incredibly crumbly with a rich slick of chocolate filling the centers.

MAKES 14–16 COOKIES

1¼ sticks (10 tablespoons) unsalted butter, slightly softened

¼ cup superfine sugar

1 egg, beaten

½ cup all-purpose flour

½ cup self-rising flour

½ cup ground almonds

1 tablespoon unsweetened cocoa powder, sifted

1 tablespoon cornstarch

Pinch of salt

FOR THE FILLING

3oz bittersweet chocolate (50% cocoa solids), broken into pieces

2 tablespoons vegetable oil

1. Preheat the oven to 350°F.

2. Cream together the butter and sugar until light and fluffy. Beat in the egg.

3. Mix the remaining cookie ingredients and gently work into the butter mixture. Refrigerate for 1 hour to harden up—it makes it easier to roll into balls.

4. Take tablespoons of the dough and form into balls. Press firmly with your thumb to make deep indentations in the centers. Place on a nonstick baking sheet and bake for 10–12 minutes until firm. Place on a wire rack to cool.

5. When the cookies have cooled, melt the chocolate in a bowl over a pan of hot water or in the microwave for 1–2 minutes. Cool a little, then stir in the oil. Pour a teaspoon of chocolate into the center of each cookie and let harden.

CHOCOLATE MADELEINES

Try and get hold of a madeleine tray—most good cookshops sell them.
It is essential to always chill a madeleine batter as the texture alters
during the resting time.

MAKES 9 MADELEINES

½ stick (4 tablespoons) sweet butter,
  melted, plus extra for greasing
  the tray
2 eggs
¼ cup superfine sugar
½ cup all-purpose flour
2 tablespoons unsweetened cocoa
  powder
1 teaspoon baking powder

1. Grease the madeleine tray with a little melted butter. Whisk the eggs and superfine sugar until really thick and pale, the whisk should leave a trail.

2. In a separate bowl sift together the flour, unsweetened cocoa, and baking powder. Fold half the flour mixture into the eggs followed by half the butter. Repeat with the remaining flour and butter.

3. Cover and chill for 30 minutes. Preheat the oven to 400°F.

4. Fill the molds with the batter and bake for 8–10 minutes until risen and firm to the touch. Let cool on a wire rack.

CHOCOLATE TIP
*Try to find silicon molds,
as it is easier to pop out the
cooked madeleines.*

CHOCOLATE SANDWICH COOKIES

Here's a pretty contrast—the dark richness of the cocoa cookies

is tempered by the mellow flavor of the vanilla buttercream filling.

MAKES **24 COOKIES**
(12 SANDWICH COOKIES)

2¼ sticks sweet butter
½ cup granulated sugar
2½ cups self-rising flour
½ cup unsweetend cocoa powder
2 tablespoons milk
FOR THE FILLING
1 stick (8 tablespoons) butter
1 cup confectioner's sugar
1 teaspoon vanilla extract

1. Preheat the oven to 350°F. Grease a baking sheet and set aside.

2. Cream the butter and sugar in a bowl until light and creamy. Sift in the flour and unsweetened cocoa, then add the milk and mix everything together until well combined.

3. With slightly damp hands, shape the dough into walnut-sized balls. Place on a greased baking sheet and press down with the back of a fork.

4. Bake in the oven for 15–20 minutes. Let cool on a wire rack.

5. For the filling, beat the butter, sugar, and vanilla extract together until smooth and creamy. Once the cookies are cold, spread a little butter cream on the flat base and sandwich together.

WHITE CHOCOLATE FINGERS

These crisp, buttery Viennese fingers are dipped in white chocolate but you could dip them in some bittersweet or milk chocolate, if you prefer.

MAKES 18 FINGERS

1¼ sticks (10 tablespoons) unsalted butter, slightly softened
⅓ cup confectioner's sugar, sifted
1 teaspoon vanilla extract
1 cup all-purose flour
3½oz white chocolate, broken into pieces

1. Preheat the oven to 350°F

2. Cream the butter, sugar, and vanilla extract until light and fluffy. Work in the flour with a wooden spoon until you have a smooth dough.

3. Spoon the mixture into a pastry bag fitted with a ¾in wide, fluted nozzle. Pipe out 3in long fingers onto a nonstick baking sheet. Leave a 2–3in gap between the cookies to allow them to spread.

4. Bake for 10–12 minutes until they are lightly golden. Leave them on the baking sheet for a few minutes to harden up before removing to a wire rack to cool completely.

5. Melt the chocolate in a bowl over a pan of hot water or in the microwave for 1–2 minutes. Dip each end of the cooled cookies in the melted chocolate and place on nonstick baking parchment until hard.

NO-BAKE CHOCOLATE BARS

These bars are incredibly easy to make and also incredibly rich—so are best cut into small squares to serve.

MAKES 8–10 SQUARES

¼ cup light brown sugar
½ cup sweetened condensed milk
¼ stick (4 tablespoons) sweet butter, slightly softened
1 cup smooth peanut butter
2 cups graham crackers, crushed
FOR THE TOPPING
8oz bittersweet chocolate (50% cocoa solids), broken into pieces
2 tablespoons vegetable oil

1. Line a 7½in square cake pan with nonstick baking parchment.

2. Place the sugar, sweetened condensed milk, butter, and peanut butter in a mixing bowl and beat until smooth. Stir in the graham cracker crumbs. Spoon into the prepared pan and level the surface. This is easiest done with your hand.

3. Melt the chocolate and oil in a bowl over a pan of hot water or in the microwave for 1–2 minutes. Let cool for 5 minutes, then stir.

4. Pour over the surface of the peanut dough and tip the pan to cover evenly. Let chill for at least 1 hour. Cut into small squares.

BASQUE CHOCOLATE CAKES

In the bakeries of the Basque region a cookie-like sponge filled with a thick custard is a very popular patisserie. Inspired by these morsels, these Basque Chocolate Cakes are a cross between a cake and a cookie with a delicious surprise of melted chocolate in the center.

MAKES 12 CAKES

3½oz bittersweet chocolate
   (70% cocoa solids),
   broken into pieces
½ stick (4 tablespoons) sweet butter
½ cup superfine sugar
1 egg, beaten
1 cup all-purpose flour
2 teaspoons baking powder
12 squares of white chocolate
   (about 2oz)
Whipping cream, to serve

1. Melt the chocolate and butter in a bowl over a pan of hot water or in the microwave for 1–2 minutes. Let cool for 5 minutes.

2. Whisk the superfine sugar and egg until light and fluffy, then stir in the cooled chocolate mixture. Mix together the flour and baking powder and fold into the chocolate. Cover and chill for at least 1 hour.

3. Preheat the oven to 325°F. Lightly grease a shallow, 12-cup muffin pan. Divide the dough in two. Take a heaped teaspoon of the chilled dough and press into the base of a muffin cup. Repeat for the remaining muffin cups.

4. Press a square of chocolate into the center of each cup, then cover with a teaspoon of dough, pressing around the edges to seal. Bake in the oven for 15 minutes, or until the cakes are firm to the touch. Remove and serve warm with some whipping cream.

DOUBLE-CHOCOLATE CHUNKY BROWNIES

Try not to overcook these moreish brownies, otherwise the soft,

gooey texture will be spoiled.

MAKES ABOUT 20 SQUARES

$2\frac{1}{4}$ sticks butter, diced, plus extra
for greasing
1lb 2oz bittersweet chocolate
1 teaspoon instant coffee granules
1 tablespoon hot water
3 large eggs
$\frac{3}{4}$ cup superfine sugar
1 teaspoon vanilla extract
$\frac{3}{4}$ cup self-rising flour
$1\frac{3}{4}$ cups pecan nuts, broken into
pieces
Unsweetened cocoa powder,
for dusting

1. Preheat the oven to 375°F. Grease and line a 8 x 12in cake pan with waxed paper.

2. Chop 6oz of the chocolate into chunks and set aside. Put the rest in a bowl with the butter and melt slowly over a pan of hot water or in the microwave for 1–2 minutes. Stir until smooth, then let cool. Meanwhile, dissolve the coffee in the hot water.

3. Lightly whisk the eggs, coffee, sugar, and vanilla extract together in a bowl. Gradually whisk in the chocolate and butter mixture, then fold in the flour, nuts, and chocolate chunks.

4. Pour into the prepared pan. Bake for 35–40 minutes or until firm to the touch.

5. Let cool for 5 minutes, then cut into squares. Cool in the pan before removing from the waxed paper. Dust with unsweetened cocoa powder before serving.

CHOCOLATE & MARSHMALLOW BLONDE BROWNIES

As the brownies cook the chocolate drops to the bottom and the melted marshmallows rise to the top.

MAKES 8–10 SQUARES

1½ sticks (tablespoons) sweet butter, slightly softened
⅔ cup light brown sugar
⅔ cup superfine sugar
3 eggs
1 teaspoon vanilla extract
1¼ cups all-purpose flour
½ teaspoon salt
1 cup bittersweet chocolate chips
1½ cups mini marshmallows or large ones cut into quarters

1. Preheat the oven to 350°F. Baseline a 8in square cake pan with nonstick baking parchment.

2. Beat together the butter and sugar until light and fluffy. Beat in the eggs and vanilla extract. Stir in the flour and salt followed by the bittersweet chocolate chips and marshmallows.

3. Spoon into the prepared pan and bake for 30–35 minutes until the center feels slightly firm to the touch. Let cool completely in the pan, then cut into squares.

MARBLED CHOCOLATE BROWNIES

The slightly salty creaminess of the cream cheese cuts through the sweetness of the chocolate. Don't expect the brownies to be completely cooked through when you take them out of the oven—they will harden up when cold. When you want to eat them, it is best to chill them and then bring them to room temperature.

MAKES 10–12 SQUARES

2$^1/_2$ sticks sweet butter
9oz bittersweet chocolate (70% cocoa solids), broken into pieces
1$^1/_2$ cups superfine sugar
4 eggs
$^3/_4$ cup all-purpose flour
$^1/_2$ teaspoon salt
11oz cream cheese

1. Preheat the oven to 350°F. Baseline a 9in square cake pan with nonstick baking parchment.

2. Melt the butter and chocolate together in a bowl over a pan of hot water or in the microwave for 1–2 minutes. Cool a little, then stir until smooth.

3. Beat the sugar with three of the eggs until they are just mixed together. Stir in the melted chocolate and butter. Fold in the flour and salt.

4. Beat the cream cheese with the remaining egg. Spoon alternate dollops of the chocolate mixture and cream cheese into the prepared pan, so you have a rough checkerboard, then swirl together for a marbled effect.

5. Bake in the oven for 45–50 minutes or until the batter stops wobbling in the center. Let cool in the pan, then refrigerate until really firm or overnight. Cut into squares and bring to room temperature to serve.

CHOCOLATE & BRAZIL NUT SHORTBREAD

Brazil nuts are one of the richest sources of selenium, so you can feel good about eating this delicious shortbread.

MAKES 8–10 WEDGES

1 stick (8 tablespoons) sweet butter
½ cup superfine sugar
1⅔ cups all-purpose flour
⅓ cup Brazil nuts, ground
2oz bittersweet chocolate
   (50–70% cocoa solids), grated

1. Preheat the oven to 325°F.

2. Cream the butter and sugar together until light and fluffy. Work in the flour, ground nuts, and grated chocolate until you have fine crumbs.

3. Press the crumb mixture into the base of a 8in loose-bottomed cake pan and level the surface. Prick with a fork, then bake in the oven for 30–35 minutes.

4. Remove from the oven and score into wedges. Let cool completely before lifting out of the pan.

TIP
When creaming butter and sugar, it is helpful to slightly soften the butter first as this will make creaming easier.

NO-BAKE MILK CHOCOLATE CRACKLE SQUARES

A great standby recipe these squares can be rustled up in a matter of minutes. If you are making these for children you might want to leave out the pine nuts.

MAKES 8–10 SQUARES

8oz milk chocolate,
   broken into pieces
¼ stick (4 tablespoons) sweet butter
1¼ cups sweetened condensed milk
3 cups rice puff cereal
¼ cup pine nuts

1. Baseline an 7 x 10in cake pan or foil tray.

2. Melt the chocolate and butter in a bowl over a pan of hot water or in the microwave for 1–2 minutes. Let cool for 10 minutes.

3. Stir in the sweetened condensed milk, then fold in the rice puffs and pine nuts. Spoon into the prepared pan, level the surface, and leave until hard—don't put the pan in the refrigerator or the cereal will go soggy.

4. Cut into squares and serve in paper cases or piled on a plate.

CHOC-MINT CUPCAKES

Any dark chocolate with a soft, fondant mint center would be fine for the frosting. These cupcakes will keep in an airtight container, however, they are best eaten within a couple of days of baking.

MAKES 12 CUPCAKES

1¼ sticks (10 tablespoons) sweet
   butter
3½oz bittersweet chocolate
   (70% cocoa solids)
   broken into pieces
¾ cup superfine sugar
2 eggs, beaten
1 cup self-rising flour
Pinch of salt
Silver balls, to decorate (optional)
FOR THE FROSTING
6oz chocolate mints
¼ cup heavy cream
½ stick (4 tablespoons) sweet butter

1. Preheat the oven to 350°F and line a 12-cup muffin pan with paper muffin cases.

2. Put the butter and chocolate in a bowl and melt over a pan of hot water or in the microwave for 1–2 minutes. Cool for a minute or two, then stir in the remaining cake ingredients.

3. Spoon a tablespoon of batter into each muffin case. Place the pan in the preheated oven and bake for 25–30 minutes until just firm to the touch. Cool on a wire rack.

4. For the frosting, place all the ingredients in a small saucepan and heat gently, stirring until smooth. Leave for a few minutes, then coat each cupcake with a tablespoon of the frosting. Let harden and, if you like, decorate with silver balls.

CHOCOLATE, COFFEE & WALNUT CUPCAKES

These cupcakes are for the grown-ups. They are moist and dark with a bitter edge of coffee.

MAKES 12 CUPCAKES

3½oz bittersweet chocolate
   (70% cocoa solids),
   broken into pieces
3 teaspoons instant coffee
   granules mixed with
   2 tablespoons boiling water
1¼ sticks (10 tablespoons) sweet
   butter
⅔ cup dark brown sugar
2 eggs
1 cup self-rising flour
¾ cup walnuts, finely chopped
Chocolate-covered coffee beans,
   to decorate (optional)

FOR THE FROSTING

2 cups confectioner's sugar, sifted
1 teaspoon instant coffee
   granules mixed with
   2 teaspoons boiling water

1. Preheat the oven to 350°F. Line a 12-cup muffin pan with paper muffin cases.

2. Put the chocolate and coffee liquid in a bowl and melt over a pan of hot water or in the microwave for 1–2 minutes. Leave for a couple of minutes to cool, then stir until smooth.

3. Cream the butter and sugar until light and fluffy and beat in the eggs. Fold in the flour followed by the melted chocolate and finally the walnuts.

4. Place a tablespoon of the batter in each paper muffin case and bake for 20 minutes or until firm to the touch. Let cool on a wire rack.

5. For the frosting, mix the confectioner's sugar with the coffee liquid and add a little more boiling water—just enough so the frosting has the consistency of heavy cream. Spoon the frosting over the cupcakes, tipping them slightly to cover the surface. Decorate with chocolate-covered coffee beans, if liked.

BLUEBERRY & WHITE CHOCOLATE MUFFINS

These muffins are delicious and so easy to make. They are especially good served warm, so heat them gently in the microwave for a few seconds before serving.

MAKES 12 MUFFINS

2 cups all-purpose flour, sifted
$\frac{2}{3}$ cups ground almonds
1 tablespoon baking powder
$\frac{1}{3}$ cup superfine sugar
1 cup milk
3 eggs, beaten
1 stick (8 tablespoons) butter, melted
$\frac{1}{2}$ teaspoon vanilla extract
$5\frac{1}{2}$oz blueberries
$2\frac{3}{4}$oz white chocolate, broken
 into small pieces
FOR THE TOPPING
$\frac{1}{2}$cup slivered almonds
2 tablespoons Turbinado sugar

1. Preheat the oven to 400°F. Line a 12-cup muffin pan with paper muffin cases.

2. Sift the flour, ground almonds, and baking powder into a large bowl and stir in the sugar. Lightly beat together the milk, eggs, and butter, then gently fold into the flour with the vanilla extract.

3. Mix in the blueberries and white chocolate pieces—the mixture should be quite lumpy so don't be tempted to beat it.

4. Spoon the mixture into the paper cases until they are three-quarters full. Top each one with a few almonds and a little Turbinado sugar, then bake until well risen and golden for 20–25 minutes.

5. Remove the muffins from the tin and let cool slightly on a wire rack before serving.

CHOCOLATE CHIP MUFFINS

These muffins are even naughtier when served drizzled with melted bittersweet chocolate!

MAKES 15 MUFFINS

3 cups self-rising flour
Pinch of salt
6 tablespoons superfine sugar
4oz good-quality bittersweet chocolate chips
½ stick (4 tablespoons) butter
6oz good-quality bittersweet chocolate, broken into pieces
2 eggs, beaten
1¼ cups buttermilk
½ cup milk

1. Preheat the oven to 425°F. Place 15 paper muffin cases into two muffin pans.

2. Mix together the flour, salt, sugar, and chocolate chips in a large bowl.

3. Melt the butter and chocolate in a bowl over a pan of hot water or in the microwave for 1–2 minutes, then let cool. Whisk in the eggs, buttermilk, and milk.

4. Combine the wet and dry ingredients and stir briskly until the flour is moistened. The mixture should appear rough and lumpy. Fill the paper muffin cases about two-thirds full. Bake for 20 minutes until risen and serve.

CHOCOLATE STREUSEL MUFFINS

The key to making good muffins is not to over-mix when combining the wet ingredients with the dry ones. It may not seem possible, but it all mixes beautifully during the cooking.

MAKES 10–12 MUFFINS

1¾ cups self-rising flour

2 teaspoons baking powder

2 tablespoons unsweetened cocoa powders

Pinch of salt

½ cup light brown sugar

2 eggs, beaten

5½oz bittersweet chocolate (50% cocoa solids)

¼ cup vegetable oil

⅔ cup milk

FOR THE STREUSEL TOPPING

¼ cup light brown sugar

⅓ cup all-purpose flour

1 tablespoon unsweetened cocoa powder, sifted

¼ stick (2 tablespoons) sweet butter

1. Preheat the oven to 375°F. Line a 12-cup muffin pan with paper muffin cases.

2. To make the streusel topping, mix the sugar, flour, and unsweetened cocoa together and rub in the butter. Set aside.

3. Mix together the flour, baking powder, unsweetened cocoa, salt, and soft brown sugar.

4. Melt the chocolate in a bowl over a pan of hot water or in the microwave for 1–2 minutes. Let cool.

5. Beat the eggs into the cooled melted chocolate along with the oil and milk. Pour the chocolate mixture into the dry ingredients and stir 3 or 4 times.

6. Spoon into the muffin cases and sprinkle generously with the streusel mixture. Bake for 15–20 minutes until just firm to the touch. Cool on a wire rack.

CHOCOLATE-COVERED DOUGHNUTS

This is a classic bakery favourite. Why not try to re-create it at home—it's easier than you think!

MAKES 8 DOUGHNUTS

2 cups all-purpose flour
1/4oz sachet fast-action dried yeast
Pinch of salt
1/4 cup superfine sugar
1/4 stick (2 tablespoons) butter
1/2 cup milk
2 egg yolks
Oil, for deep-frying
2oz milk chocolate,
   broken into pieces

1. Mix the flour with the yeast and salt. Add the superfine sugar, then rub in the butter until the mixture resembles fine breadcrumbs.

2. Heat the milk until it is warm. Whisk in the egg yolks, then add the liquid to the flour. Mix to form a soft dough. Cover the bowl with plastic wrap and leave in a warm place for about an hour or until the dough has doubled in size.

3. Knock back the dough on a well-floured surface for 5–10 minutes. Roll out the dough to 1/2in thick and stamp out rounds with a plain cookie cutter. Make a hole in the middle of each round with your finger. Place the doughnuts on a greased tray and leave to double in size.

4. Deep-fry the doughnuts in hot oil for about 5 minutes or until they are golden brown. Drain on kitchen paper and let cool.

5. Melt the chocolate in a bowl over a pan of hot water or in the microwave for 1–2 minutes. Let cool slightly.

6. Dip the rounded tops of the doughnuts in the melted chocolate and let harden.

CHOCOLATE BRIOCHE LOAF

Brioche, beloved by the French, is a rich, slightly sweet bread.
Delicious served at breakfast or at teatime.

MAKES 8–10 SLICES

2 cups strong flour
Pinch of salt
¼ cup superfine sugar
2 teaspoons (about ¼oz)
   fast-action dried yeast
½ stock (4 tablespoons) sweet butter
2 eggs, beaten
¼ cup warm milk
2oz bittersweet chocolate morsels
FOR THE GLAZE
1 egg beaten with
   1 tablespoon water

1. Mix together the flour, salt, sugar, and yeast. Heat the butter in a small saucepan until it has just melted but don't let it boil. Let cool a little.

2. Mix the eggs and warm milk together and pour into the flour, followed by the cooled butter. Bring the mixture together to form a smooth dough and knead by hand for 10 minutes or with a dough hook in a food processor or blender for 5 minutes.

3. Turn into a lightly oiled mixing bowl, cover with oiled plastic wrap and let rise in a warm place for about an hour or until it has doubled in size.

4. Preheat the oven to 400°F. Grease a fluted brioche mold.

5. Turn the dough out onto a floured surface and knock out the air. Knead in the chocolate morsels. Shape into a round and place in the well-buttered brioche 2.5 pint mold. Let rise in a warm place for 15–20 minutes.

6. Brush the surface with a thin layer of the egg glaze, then bake in the oven for 15 minutes. Turn the heat down to 350°F and continue to bake for a further 15 minutes.

7. Let cool in the tin for 5 minutes, then turn out onto a wire rack to cool completely.

CHOCOLATE CINNAMON SWIRL LOAF

This is a rich freeform dough with veins and swirls of chocolate and cinnamon running through it giving it just a touch of sweetness.

MAKES 10–12 SLICES

5 cups strong flour
1 teaspoon salt
¼ cup superfine sugar
4 teaspoons fast-action
   dried yeast
1¼ cups milk
¾ stick (6 tablespoons) sweet butter
3 eggs, beaten
3½oz bittersweet chocolate
   (70% cocoa solids), grated
2 teaspoons ground cinnamon
⅓ cup light brown sugar

FOR THE GLAZE

1 cup confectioner's sugar, sifted
¼ cup unsweetened cocoa powder,
   sifted

1. Mix together the flour, salt, superfine sugar, and yeast in a large mixing bowl.

2. Put the milk and butter in a saucepan and heat slowly until the butter has melted but don't let the milk boil. Cool a little, then stir in the beaten eggs.

3. Add the warm liquid to the flour mixture and bring everything together to form a smooth dough. Either knead by hand for 10 minutes or with a dough hook in a food processor or blender for 5 minutes.

4. Turn into a large, lightly oiled mixing bowl, cover with oiled plastic wrap and let rise in a warm place for about an hour or until it has doubled in size.

5. Mix together the grated chocolate, cinnamon, and soft brown sugar. Turn the risen dough out onto a well-floured surface, knock out the air, and knead for 5 minutes.

6. Roll out the dough to a large rectangle about 16 x 10in. Scatter the grated chocolate mixture over the surface, then roll up to form a long sausage. Curl the sausage into a snail shape and lay in the base of a 10in buttered cake pan.

7. Preheat the oven to 400°F. Leave the dough to rise in a warm place for 15–20 minutes, then bake in the oven for 15 minutes.

8. Reduce the heat to 325°F and continue to bake for 25–30 minutes. The dough should sound hollowed when tapped. Leave in the tin for 10 minutes, then turn out onto a wire rack to cool completely.

9. When the bread is cold make the glaze. Mix the confectioner's sugar and unsweetened cocoa together and stir in 1–2 tablespoons hot water. The glaze should be the consistency of heavy cream. Drizzle over the surface of the loaf, letting it drip down the sides.

TIP

Using a dough hook attached to a food processor takes the effort out of bread making, it takes slightly less time, and still gives excellent results. Whether kneading the dough by hand or using a dough hook, you are looking for a dough that is smooth, elastic and no longer sticky. Kneading dough is the most critical stage of bread making. It is when the gluten in the flour is activated.

EASY PAIN AU CHOCOLAT

Perhaps not the real McCoy but delicious all the same—quick, easy, and the perfect accompaniment to a hot cup of tea as a mid-morning snack or to a scoop of vanilla ice cream as a dessert.

MAKES 6 PASTRIES

8oz ready-made puff pastry,
    preferably all-butter
12 squares bittersweet chocolate
    (50% cocoa solids), about 3½oz
1 egg, beaten
2 tablespoons confectioner's sugar,
    sieved

1. Roll out the dough into a rectangle 11 x 14in. Cut into three strips lengthwise, then cut across the middle horizontally so you end up with six rectangles about 4 x 7in.

2. Place two squares of chocolate just above the middle of each rectangle and bring the bottom edge up to the top edge. Then fold the two edges back down to the middle. Turn the pastries over and place on a baking sheet lined with nonstick baking parchment. Chill for 15 minutes. Preheat the oven to 350°F.

3. Brush the pastries with beaten egg and dust with the confectioner's sugar. Bake for 15–20 minutes until puffed up and golden. Let cool for 10 minutes before serving.

CHOCOLATE PANETTONE

Panettone is a sweet Italian bread traditionally flavored with candied fruit and raisins. Here bittersweet chocolate morsels are also added for an extra rich treat. As the dough has so much butter incorporated it takes nearly double the time to rise, so allow plenty of time.

MAKES 12–16 SLICES

4 cups strong all-purpose flour
1 teaspoon salt
½ cup superfine sugar
2 teaspoons (about ¼oz)
    fast-action dried yeast
Grated rind of 2 oranges
2 eggs beaten with 2 egg yolks
½ cup warm milk
1¾ sticks (14 tablespoons) sweet
    butter, softened
2oz candied peel, diced
2¾oz plain chocolate morsels
2oz raisins

1. Line a deep 8in cake pan with baking parchment that comes 2in above the top of the pan.

2. Mix together the flour, salt, sugar, yeast, and orange rind. Mix the eggs with the warm milk and pour into the flour mixture. Stir well and bring together to form a smooth dough. Gradually beat in the softened butter. This is easiest done in a food processor with a dough hook. Knead for 5–10 minutes.

3. Place the dough in a lightly oiled mixing bowl, cover with oiled plastic wrap and let rise and double in size. This will take about 2 hours.

4. Turn the dough out onto a floured surface and knock out the air. Knead in the candied peel, chocolate morsels, and raisins. Form into a round and place in the cake pan. Leave for 50–60 minutes to rise. Preheat the oven to 400°F.

5. Bake the panettone in the oven for 15 minutes, then turn the heat down to 350°F and bake for a further 35–40 minutes. If the dough starts to brown too much cover with a piece of aluminum foil.

6. Let cool in the pan for 10 minutes, then turn out onto a wire rack to cool completely.

CHOCOLATE BANANA BREAD

A quick and easy bread, which is delicious served on its own or with butter, to rustle up for a teatime treat. Make sure the bananas are really ripe or the flavor won't be so good.

MAKES 12–14 SLICES

1½ cups all-purpose flour
2 teaspoons baking powder
½ teaspoon salt
1 teaspoon ground mixed spice
1 stick (8 tablespoons) sweet butter
⅔ cup superfine sugar
2 eggs, beaten
1 teaspoon vanilla extract
3 ripe bananas (about 1lb), mashed
3½oz bittersweet chocolate morsels

1. Preheat the oven to 350°F. Grease and baseline a 2.25lb loaf pan.

2. Mix together the flour, baking powder, salt, and ground mixed spice.

3. Cream the butter and sugar until light and fluffy. Beat in the eggs and vanilla extract followed by the mashed bananas. Fold into the flour mixture and then fold in the chocolate morsels.

4. Spoon into the prepared pan and bake for 1½ hours or until the loaf feels firm to the touch.

5. Let cool in the pan for 20 minutes, then turn out onto a wire rack to cool completely. This bread will keep for 4–5 days in an airtight container.

THE
PATISSERIE

CHOCOLATE & RASPBERRY ROULADE

This is a perfect afternoon tea treat—just sweet and creamy enough to keep you going through the rest of the day.

MAKES 6–8 SLICES

6oz good-quality bittersweet chocolate, broken into pieces
$\frac{1}{3}$ cup water
1 tablespoon instant coffee granules
5 eggs, separated
$\frac{2}{3}$ cup superfine sugar
$\frac{3}{4}$ cup heavy cream, whipped
5oz fresh raspberries
Confectioner's sugar, for dusting

1. Preheat the oven to 400°F. Line a large $8\frac{1}{2}$ x 13in jelly roll pan with nonstick baking parchment.

2. Melt the chocolate, water, and coffee in a bowl over a pan of hot water or in the microwave for 1–2 minutes. Let cool slightly.

3. Combine the egg yolks and superfine sugar and whisk until thick and fluffy. Stir in the melted chocolate. Beat the egg whites to soft peaks and carefully fold into the chocolate mixture.

4. Pour into the jelly roll pan and bake in the oven for 10–12 minutes until firm. Turn out onto another piece of baking parchment and cover with a damp dish towel. Let cool.

5. Spread the whipped cream over the sponge, evenly scatter the raspberries on top, and roll up. Dust with confectioner's sugar just before serving.

CHOCOLATE CHIP CHIFFON CAKE

A chiffon cake is characteristically baked in a deep ring mold. It is light and airy—a bit like an angel food cake.

MAKES 8–10 SLICES

2½ cups all-purpose flour
1 tablespoon baking powder
½ teaspoon salt
1⅓ cups superfine sugar
6 eggs, separated,
    plus 1 extra egg white
⅓ cup vegetable oil
½ cup water
1 teaspoon vanilla extract
½ teaspoon cream of tartar
6oz bittersweet chocolate chips

1. Preheat the oven to 325°F. Liberally grease a deep savarin ring mold or kugelhopf mold with butter.

2. In a large bowl mix together the flour, baking powder, salt, and sugar. Mix together the egg yolks, oil, water, and vanilla extract, then stir into the flour mixture. Beat for 1 minute.

3. Whisk the egg whites with the cream of tartar until stiff but not dry. Fold into the batter along with the chocolate chips.

4. Pour into the prepared mold and bake for 50–55 minutes or until firm to the touch. Turn onto a wire rack to cool completely.

CHOCOLATE PRALINE TORTE

MAKES 8–10 SLICES

FOR THE PRALINE
1 cup blanched almonds
½ cup superfine sugar

FOR THE TORTE
6oz bittersweet chocolate
    (50% cocoa solids),
    broken into pieces
1 stick (8 tablespoons) sweet butter
4 eggs, separated
⅓ cup superfine sugar
⅓ cup all-purpose flour

FOR THE FROSTING
1 cup heavy cream
1 tablespoon sweet butter
7oz praline-flavored milk chocolate
    (e.g. Guylian shells), broken into
    pieces

NOTE
This recipe makes more praline than you will need in the recipe. However, it keeps well in an airtight container.

1. Preheat the oven to 375°F. Grease and baseline a 8in springform cake pan.

2. For the praline, place the almonds in a large skillet and toast over a gentle heat, turning frequently for 4–5 minutes until golden. Set aside.

3. Place the sugar and 4 tablespoons water in the skillet and over a very low heat let the sugar dissolve. Turn the heat up slightly, add the almonds, and allow the mixture to cook until a golden caramel color. Immediately pour onto an oiled baking sheet and let cool and harden.

4. Roughly break up the praline and place in a food processor or blender. Keep a few shards aside for decoration. Pulse until you have fine breadcrumbs.

5. For the torte, melt the chocolate and butter over a pan of hot water or in the microwave for 1–2 minutes. Let cool a little, then stir to combine.

6. Beat together the egg yolks and sugar until light, thick, and the whisk leaves a trail. Fold in the chocolate mixture, 3½oz praline, and then the flour.

7. Whisk the egg whites until they form soft peaks. Fold into the chocolate mixture, then pour into the prepared pan. Bake for 25–30 minutes or until just firm to the touch. Take out of the oven and let cool in the pan.

8. For the frosting, heat the cream and butter in a pan and just as it is coming up to a boil add the chocolate. Stir until the chocolate has melted then let cool. Chill until quite cold, then beat until the mixture is stiff and holds its shape. Cover the torte with the frosting, sprinkle with roughly chopped praline, and chill until firm.

CHOCOLATE PRUNE CAKE

This is a very moist, flourless cake that will keep well for 4–5 days.

MAKES 8–10 SLICES

5½oz plain chocolate
(50% cocoa solids),
broken into pieces
½ stick (4 tablespoons) sweet butter
9oz pitted prunes, puréed with a
couple of tablespoons hot water
4 eggs, separated
¼ cup superfine sugar
Whipping cream, to serve

1. Preheat the oven to 350°F. Grease and baseline a 8in springform cake pan.

2. Melt the chocolate and butter in a bowl over a pan of hot water or in the microwave for 1–2 minutes. Cool a little and then stir in the prune purée.

3. Whisk the egg yolks with the sugar until light and fluffy and thick. Fold the chocolate and prune mixture into the egg yolks.

4. Whisk the egg whites to soft peaks and fold into the chocolate. Pour into the prepared pan and bake for 30 minutes or until firm to the touch.

5. Let cool in the pan, then turn out. Serve with whipping cream.

WHITE CHOCOLATE, PEAR & ALMOND CAKE

You could use dried cherries or blueberries instead of the nuts, if you prefer.

MAKES 8–10 SLICES

1 ripe pear
1¾ sticks (14 tablespoons) sweet butter, slightly softened
¾ cup superfine sugar
3 eggs
2 teaspoons vanilla extract
1½ cups all-purpose flour
1 teaspoon baking powder
5½ oz white chocolate, finely chopped
⅓ cup blanched almonds, roughly chopped
Confectioner's sugar, for dusting

1. Preheat the oven to 350°F. Grease and baseline a 8in cake pan.

2. Peel and core the pear and cut into eighths.

3. Cream the butter and sugar together until light and fluffy. Gradually beat in the eggs and vanilla extract.

4. Fold in the flour and baking powder, and finally the white chocolate and almonds.

5. Spoon the cake mixture into the prepared pan and level the surface. Place the pears in a circle on top, pressing them down into the batter. Bake for 45–50 minutes or until risen and firm in the center.

6. Let cool in the pan for 10 minutes before removing and cooling on a wire rack. Dust with confectioner's sugar to serve.

SACHERTORTE

This famous Austrian cake originates in Vienna, where all the cafés claim to make the best one. Some recipes call for almond essence, but I prefer not to use it.

MAKES 8–10 SLICES

6oz bittersweet chocolate
  (70% cocoa solids),
  broken into pieces
1 stick (8 tablespoons) sweet butter
3/4 cup sugar
5 eggs, separated
1 cup all-purpose flour

FOR THE GLAZE
3 tablespoons apricot jelly

FOR THE FROSTING
2/3 cup superfine sugar
3 1/2oz bittersweet chocolate
  (70% cocoa solids),
  broken into pieces
6 tablespoons water

1. Preheat the oven to 325°F. Line a 8in cake pan with nonstick baking parchment.

2. Melt the chocolate in a bowl over a pan of hot water or in the microwave for 1–2 minutes.

3. Beat the butter and sugar together, then beat in the egg yolks. Stir in the melted chocolate.

4. Beat the egg whites to soft-peak stage and carefully fold into the chocolate mixture.

5. Sift the flour over and fold in trying to keep as much air as possible in the mixture. Spoon into the prepared pan and bake for 40–45 minutes or until a skewer inserted into the middle comes out clean. Let cool in the pan, then place on a wire rack.

6. For the glaze, heat the apricot jelly with a tablespoon of water. If lumpy, pass through a strainer. Cool a little, then brush the glaze over the cake.

7. For the frosting, place the ingredients in a saucepan and heat through until the sugar has dissolved and the chocolate melted. Then turn the heat up and boil until the temperature reaches 221°F on a sugar thermometer, just below jelly stage. Remove from the heat and stir for 1 minute. Pour evenly over the cake. Smooth round the sides with a palette knife, but don't touch the top or it will lose its glossy sheen.

CHOCOLATE KUGELHOPF

A kugelhopf is normally a yeasted bread eaten for breakfast in Germany. Here it is a marbled cake, which is baked in the traditional fluted dome-shaped mold. It is quite a light, dry cake, which is why it is so popular for breakfast.

MAKES 8–10 SLICES

3½oz bittersweet chocolate
(70% cocoa solids),
broken into pieces
⅓ cup ground almonds
1⅔ cups all-purpose flour mixed with
1 teaspoon baking powder
3 eggs
¾ cup superfine sugar
1 teaspoon vanilla extract
FOR THE FROSTING
1 cup confectioner's sugar, sifted
¼ cup unsweetened cocoa powder,
sifted

TIP
This cake is easily doubled and you can use the same sized pan (see picture). Increase the cooking time by 45 minutes. Test if cooked with a skewer, which should come out clean – it may need another 5 minutes.

1. Preheat the oven to 300°F and liberally butter a 3 pint kugelhopf mold.

2. Melt the chocolate in a bowl over a pan of hot water or in the microwave for 1–2 minutes. Let cool slightly, then stir.

3. Mix the ground almonds with the flour. Beat the eggs, sugar, and vanilla extract until very light and bulky, about 5 minutes.

4. Carefully fold in the flour mixture trying to keep as much air in the batter as possible. Pour in the chocolate and stir—just a couple of times to get a marble effect.

5. Spoon into the prepared mold and bake for 30 minutes or until firm to the touch.

6. Let cool for 10 minutes in the mould, then turn out onto a wire rack to cool completely.

7. Mix the confectioner's sugar and cocoa powder together and add just enough hot water to get a thick pouring consistency. Drizzle over the cake.

SOUR CREAM CHOCOLATE CAKE

To ring the changes I like to bake this in a loaf pan. You can cover the cake in a frosting of your choice but I happen to like it plain.

MAKES 12–14 SLICES

7oz bittersweet chocolate
(60% cocoa solids or a mixture
of half 50% and half 70%),
broken into pieces
1 stick (8 tablespoons) sweet butter,
slightly softened
$^2/_3$ cup superfine sugar
3 eggs
1 cup sour cream or crème fraîche
$1^1/_4$ cup all-purpose flour
1 teaspoon baking powder
Pinch of salt
Frosting and chocolate leaves,
to decorate (optional)

1. Preheat the oven to 325°F. Grease and baseline a $2^1/_4$lb loaf pan with nonstick baking parchment.

2. Melt the chocolate in a bowl over a pan of hot water or in the microwave for 1–2 minutes. Let cool slightly, then stir.

3. Cream the butter and sugar until light and fluffy. Beat in the eggs, then stir in the sour cream or crème fraîche and the melted chocolate.

4. Mix the flour and baking powder together with the pinch of salt and fold into the batter.

5. Spoon the mixture into the pan, level the surface, and bake in the oven for 40–45 minutes or until a skewer inserted into the middle comes out just clean.

6. Let cool in the pan for 15 minutes, then turn out onto a wire rack. Either leave plain or cover with frosting and decorate with chocolate leaves, if liked (see page 13).

CHOCOLATE POUND CAKE

A lot of the recipes in this chapter are very dense chocolatey cakes, but this one is a light, hint-of-chocolate cake. I like to drizzle a little glacé icing over the top to serve.

MAKES 8–10 SLICES

3¹⁄₂oz bittersweet chocolate
   (50% cocoa solids),
   broken into pieces
2 sticks sweet butter, softened
1 cup superfine sugar
4 eggs
5¹⁄₂oz plain yogurt
1 teaspoon vanilla extract
2¹⁄₃ cups self-rising flour
Glacé icing (optional) (see page 154)

1. Preheat the oven to 325°F. Grease and baseline a 8in cake pan.

2. Melt the chocolate in a bowl over a pan of hot water or in the microwave for 1–2 minutes. Let cool a little.

3. Cream the butter and sugar together until light and fluffy. Beat in the eggs followed by the yogurt, vanilla extract, and melted chocolate. Fold in the flour.

4. Spoon the mixture into the pan and bake for 50–55 minutes or until a skewer inserted into the middle comes out clean.

5. Leave to cool in the tin for 10 minutes, then turn out onto a wire rack to cool completely. When cold drizzle with glacé icing if you like.

WHITE CHOCOLATE CAPPUCCINO CAKE

White chocolate can be a bit sickly but the bitterness of the coffee cuts through the sweetness. I think it works best sandwiched with slightly sweetened whipping cream, but you could use an frosting of your choice.

MAKES 6–8 SLICES

4½oz white chocolate, broken into pieces
3 tablespoons milk
1½ sticks (12 tablespoons) sweet butter, slightly softened
¾ cup light brown sugar
3 eggs
2 teaspoons instant coffee granules mixed with 2 tablespoons boiling water
1½ cups self-rising flour
⅔ cup heavy cream
¼oz confectioner's sugar, plus extra for dusting

1. Preheat the oven to 350°F. Grease and baseline two 7in sandwich pans.

2. Melt the chocolate with the milk in a bowl over a pan of hot water or in the microwave for 1–2 minutes. Let cool a little, then stir.

3. Cream the butter and sugar together until light and fluffy. Gradually beat in the eggs and then the coffee liquid.

4. Stir in the melted chocolate. Mix well and then finally, fold in the flour.

5. Divide the mixture between the two prepared pans and bake for 20–25 minutes until golden and firm to the touch. Turn out onto a wire rack and let cool.

6. When the cake has cooled, whip together the cream and confectioner's sugar until it is holding its shape and spread over one half of the cake. Top with the remaining half and dust the top liberally with confectioner's sugar.

CHOCOLATE CHESTNUT CAKE

This rich, intense, flourless cake could just as well be served as a pudding.
Just add whipping cream to serve.

MAKES 8–10 SLICES

9oz bittersweet chocolate
   (70% cocoa solids),
   broken into pieces
1 stick (8 tablespoons) sweet butter
5 eggs, separated
⅓ cup light brown sugar
2 cups sweetened chestnut purée

1. Preheat the oven to 350°F. Grease and baseline a 8in springform cake pan.

2. Melt the chocolate and butter in a bowl over a pan of hot water or in the microwave for 1–2 minutes. Let cool slightly, then stir until the mixture is smooth.

3. Beat the egg yolks with the sugar until thick. Stir into the melted chocolate mixture followed by the chestnut purée.

4. Whisk the egg whites until they are stiff but not dry and fold into the chocolate mixture.

5. Pour into the prepared pan and bake for 40–45 minutes. Let cool in the pan.

NO-BAKE CHOCOLATE LAYER CAKE

I use ginger cookies here, but you could substitute a Graham cracker or shortbread if you aren't too keen on the flavor of ginger. You could also use a wheat or gluten-free cookies if you are intolerant.

MAKES 10–12 SLICES

10½oz bittersweet chocolate
  (50% cocoa solids),
  broken into pieces
1 stick (8 tablespoons) sweet butter,
  cut into small pieces
14oz can sweetened condensed milk
4oz ginger cookies or similar,
  roughly broken

1. Baseline a 2-pint loaf pan with nonstick baking parchment.

2. Melt the chocolate in a bowl over a pan of hot water or in the microwave for 1–2 minutes. Let cool a little, then stir until smooth.

3. Gradually add the pieces of butter, beating them in until they have melted and the mixture is smooth. Stir in the condensed milk.

4. Pour a third of the chocolate mixture into the base of the pan. Arrange half the broken cookies in a single layer over the chocolate. Cover with another third of chocolate and repeat with the remaining cookies. Pour over the rest of the chocolate.

5. Cover with plastic wrap and place in the refrigerator to firm up for about 2–3 hours. Loosen the edges of the layer cake with a sharp knife and turn out onto a plate to serve.

CHOCOLATE FUDGE CAKE

A real fudgy treat here that creates quite a focal point with its many layers of decadence.

MAKES 8 SLICES

1¾ sticks (14 tablespoons) sweet
   butter, plus extra for greasing
9oz bittersweet chocolate,
   (70% cocoa solids), broken
   into pieces
4 tablespoons water
¾ cup light brown sugar
4 eggs, beaten
1 cup self-rising flour
1 cup ground almonds
Melted milk chocolate,
   to decorate (optional)

FOR THE FILLING

½ cup unsweetened cocoa powder
¾ cup light brown sugar
⅓ cup confectioner's sugar
1¾ sticks (14 tablespoons) sweet
   butter, melted
4 tablespoons boiling water

FOR THE FROSTING

4oz bittersweet chocolate,
   broken into pieces
½ stick (4 tablespoons) sweet butter
Melted milk chocolate, for decoration
   (optional)

1. Preheat the oven to 350°F. Grease and baseline two 7in cake pans.

2. Melt the chocolate with the water in a bowl over a pan of hot water or in the microwave for 1–2 minutes. Let cool slightly.

3. Cream the butter and sugar together until light and fluffy. Gradually add the beaten eggs. Stir in the melted chocolate, then fold in the flour and ground almonds. Pour into the prepared cake pans.

4. Bake for 25 minutes. Let cool a little, then turn out both cake halves onto a wire rack. With a long sharp knife, slice them through the middle horizontally so you have four layers.

5. For the filling, mix the cocoa powder, brown sugar, and confectioner's sugar together. Beat in the melted butter and stir in the water to make a smooth paste. Let harden in the refrigerator for about 20 minutes, then spread evenly over three layers of the cake and sandwich together. Put the final cake layer on top.

6. For the frosting, melt the bittersweet chocolate and butter together in a bowl over a pan of hot water or in the microwave for 1–2 minutes. Beat until glossy, then let cool until you have a spreading consistency. Smooth evenly over the top of the cake. Drizzle melted milk chocolate over in zigzag patterns, if liked.

SOFT & GOOEY CHOCOLATE CAKE

This is a cake that is best made 24 hours in advance as it needs to firm up a bit before serving.

MAKES 10–12 SLICES

9oz bittersweet chocolate
   (70% cocoa solids),
   broken into pieces
2¼ sticks (1 cup) sweet butter
3oz corn syrup
5 eggs
¾ cup superfine sugar
½ cup all-purpose flour
Crème fraîche or sour cream,
   to serve

1. Preheat the oven to 300°F. Grease and baseline a 9in springform cake pan with nonstick baking parchment.

2. Melt the chocolate, butter, and corn syrup in a bowl over a pan of hot water or in the microwave for 1–2 minutes. Cool a little, then stir until smooth.

3. In a large bowl stir together the eggs, superfine sugar and flour just until the mixture is smooth. Stir in the cooled chocolate mixture. Pour into the prepared pan.

4. Bake for 25–30 minutes—the cake will still have a slight wobble in the middle. Remove from the oven and leave in the pan to cool.

5. Remove the sides of the springform pan but leave the cake on its base and chill for at least an hour. It should be firm enough to slip off the base of the pan. Bring to room temperature and serve with crème fraîche or sour cream.

CHOCOLATE POLENTA CAKE

The polenta in this flourless cake gives it a lovely texture. You can also use fine semolina if you can't find fine polenta.

MAKES 10–12 SLICES

8oz bittersweet chocolate
  (60% cocoa solids),
  broken into pieces
1/2 stick (4 tablespoons) sweet butter
5 eggs, separated
1/2 cup superfine sugar
4oz fine polenta
Unsweetened cocoa powder,
  for dusting
Confectioner's sugar, for dusting

1. Preheat the oven to 350°F. Grease and baseline a 9in springform cake pan.

2. Melt the chocolate with the butter in a bowl over a pan of hot water or in the microwave for 1–2 minutes. Let cool slightly, then gently stir until smooth.

3. Whisk the egg yolks with half the sugar until pale and bulky, then stir in the chocolate mixture. Sprinkle the polenta over the mixture and fold in.

4. Whisk the egg whites with the remaining sugar until stiff peaks form, and then fold into the cake batter. Pour into the prepared pan and bake for 25–30 minutes or until slightly firm to the touch.

5. Leave in the pan to cool, then turn out. Dust with unsweetened cocoa powder and confectioner's sugar to serve.

HAZELNUT MERINGUE LAYER CAKE

MAKES 8–10 SLICES

6 eggs, separated
1½ cups superfine sugar
1 teaspoon wine vinegar
2 cups ground hazelnuts,
   lightly toasted
12oz bittersweet chocolate
   (50% cocoa solids),
   broken into pieces
1 cup confectioner's sugar, sifted
2½ cups whipping cream
Caramel sauce (optional)
Unsweetened cocoa powder,
   for dusting

TIP

*This cake can also be
served as a pudding. You can
make and assemble it in advance,
then freeze it whole. Defrost
at room temperature
for 4–5 hours.*

1. Preheat the oven to 250°F. Line three baking sheets with nonstick baking parchment and mark out a 8in diameter circle on each.

2. Beat the egg whites until stiff then beat in half the superfine sugar a tablespoon at a time. Fold in the remaining superfine sugar followed by the vinegar and ground hazelnuts.

3. Evenly distribute the meringue between the drawn-out discs and level the surfaces so you have three flat discs. Bake in the oven for 1–1½ hours. Remove and place the discs on a wire rack to cool completely.

4. Melt the chocolate in a bowl over a pan of hot water or in the microwave for 1–2 minutes. Let cool a little.

5. Place the egg yolks in a large mixing bowl and whisk in the confectioner's sugar until the mixture has doubled in bulk. Stir in the cooled chocolate.

6. Whisk the cream until it is just holding its shape and stir in a couple of tablespoons to soften up the chocolate mixture. Fold in the rest and then chill until the mousse is firm enough to spread, about 2 hours.

7. Spoon half of the chocolate over one meringue disc and smooth to the edges. Lay another meringue disc on top and repeat with the remaining chocolate mousse. Top with the final disc and dust with cocoa powder. If liked, drizzle over each layout of chocolate mousse your favorite caramel sauce. Chill for 1 hour before serving or wrap and freeze.

CHOCOLATE CRATER CAKE

This is a flourless cake—a sort of sunken soufflé that you can fill with whipped cream.

MAKES 8–10 SLICES

8oz bittersweet chocolate
   (70% cocoa solids),
   broken into pieces
1 stick (8 tablespoons) sweet butter
4 eggs, separated
½ cup superfine sugar
1 teaspoon bitter almond essence
Unsweetened cocoa powder,
   for dusting

1. Preheat the oven to 350°F. Place a roasting pan of boiling water in the bottom of the oven. Grease and baseline a 8in springform cake pan.

2. Melt the chocolate and butter in a bowl over a pan of hot water or in the microwave for 1–2 minutes. Let cool a little, then gently stir until smooth.

3. Beat the egg yolks, superfine sugar, and almond extract until really light and creamy. Fold in the chocolate mixture.

4. Whisk the egg whites until stiff and fold into the chocolate mixture. Pour into the prepared pan and bake for 25–30 minutes.

5. Remove from the oven and let cool in the pan. This is a very fragile cake so it is best not to try and remove it from its base. Dust with unsweetened cocoa powder before serving.

SPICED CHOCOLATE CAKE

This is a dense chocolate cake with a hint of spice. It is delicious sliced and spread with a little butter.

MAKES 10–12 SLICES

5½oz bittersweet chocolate
   (70% cocoa solids),
   broken into pieces
1 stick (8 tablespoons) sweet butter
3oz corn syrup
3 cups all-purpose flour
2 teaspoons baking powder
1 tablespoon ground cinnamon
2 teaspoons ground ginger
½ teaspoon freshly grated nutmeg
2 eggs
½ cup dark brown sugar
½ cup heavy cream

1. Preheat the oven to 300°F. Grease and baseline a 9in square cake pan.

2. Melt the chocolate with the butter and corn syrup in a bowl over a pan of hot water or in the microwave for 1–2 minutes. Let cool a little, then stir until smooth.

3. Mix together the flour, baking powder, and spices in a bowl.

4. Beat the eggs and sugar together until pale and thick. Stir in the melted chocolate mixture, then fold in the flour. Stir in the heavy cream.

5. Spoon into the prepared pan and bake for 35 minutes or until a skewer inserted into the middle comes out clean. Leave to cool in the pan for 5 minutes, then turn out onto a wire rack to cool completely.

THE DESSERT TROLLEY

MARSHMALLOW & CHOCOLATE ICE CREAM

This rich, luxurious ice cream is even more indulgent when drizzled with a rich chocolate sauce.

SERVES 8

9oz milk chocolate,
  broken into pieces
7oz marshmallows, plus extra
  to decorate (optional)
3 tablespoons water
2 x 14oz cartons fresh custard sauce
1¼ cups heavy cream
Rich bittersweet chocolate sauce
  (see page 148), to serve (optional)

1. Place the chocolate in a heatproof bowl with three-quarters of the marshmallows. Add the water and set the bowl over a pan of hot water or melt in the microwave for 1–2 minutes. Melt the chocolate and stir until smooth, then let cool a little.

2. Stir the cooled chocolate mixture into the custard sauce. Chop the remaining marshmallows and fold into the mixture, then lightly whip the cream and fold in.

3. Pour the mixture into a 2½ pint terrine or loaf pan and freeze until hard. You may want to line the bottom of the pan with nonstick baking parchment to make it easier to unmold.

4. To serve, dip the base of the mold in hot water and invert on a serving plate. Cut the ice cream into thick slices, decorate with marshmallows, and served with chocolate sauce, if liked.

WHITE CHOCOLATE SEMI-FREDDO

Semi-freddo is an Italian dessert—a light and airy ice cream that is not churned and is eaten just on the point of setting. You can make this a few days in advance, but leave it at room temperature for about 45 minutes before you eat it. However, as with all things containing fresh eggs, remember not to refreeze it.

SERVES 6

7oz white chocolate,
    broken into pieces
4 eggs, separated
⅓ cup superfine sugar
1¾ cups heavy cream

1. Melt the chocolate in a bowl over a pan of hot water or in the microwave for 1–2 minutes. Let cool.

2. Whisk the egg yolks with the sugar until really thick and bulky. Stir a little of the egg yolk mixture into the chocolate, then fold in the rest.

3. In another bowl whisk the cream until it is just holding soft peaks. Stir into the chocolate and egg yolk mixture.

4. Finally beat the egg whites to stiff peaks and fold in. Pour the mixture into a container or into individual serving bowls and freeze for 4–5 hours or until the semi-freddo is on the point of setting.

BITTER CHOCOLATE SORBET

Intensely dark and rich, this will satisfy your chocolate cravings. The chocolate must be a good brand and contain at least 70% cocoa solids or the finished sorbet will suffer as a result.

SERVES 4

8oz bittersweet chocolate
   (at least 70% cocoa solids)
1 cup sugar
¼ cup unsweetened cocoa powder

1. Put the chocolate in a food processor and blend until finely chopped. Place the sugar and cocoa in a saucepan with 2 cups water and slowly bring to a boil, stirring to dissolve the sugar. Simmer for 5 minutes.

2. Pour the chocolate syrup into the food processor and run until the mixture is completely smooth and the chocolate has melted. Pour into a shallow container and let cool. Once cool, put in the freezer to harden for 2–3 hours.

3. Remove from the freezer. Blend until smooth in the food processor, then return to the container and freeze until hard.

CHOCOLATE AFFOGATO

Affogato is a wonderful instant dessert—and easy to make to finish any dinner party. Normally a shot of fresh espresso coffee is poured over a scoop or two of vanilla ice cream. Here the addition of a little rich chocolate fudge sauce makes this a real treat.

SERVES 6

1 quantity of sticky chocolate
   fudge sauce (see page 150)
12 scoops good-quality
   vanilla ice cream
6 shots of hot espresso coffee

1. Pour the chocolate sauce into six sundae glasses or pudding bowls.

2. Place 2 scoops vanilla ice cream on top of each and finally pour over the hot coffee. Serve immediately.

TIP
For a double hit of coffee you can substitute the vanilla ice cream for a coffee one. For contrast, add a dollop of whipped cream on the top.

CHOCOLATE CHIP & COCONUT ICE CREAM

This creamy ice cream with a subtle taste of coconut has the delightful contrast of crunchy plain chocolate chips.

SERVES 4

2³/₄ cups coconut milk
5 egg yolks
³/₄ cup sugar
³/₄ cup whipping cream
5¹/₂oz bittersweet chocolate chips

1. Place the coconut milk in a saucepan and slowly bring to a boil.

2. Meanwhile in a bowl whisk the egg yolks and sugar together. Pour over the hot milk and stir. Strain through a strainer and pour back into the saucepan.

3. Stir over a gentle heat until the custard just coats the back of a wooden spoon. Pour into a bowl, cover, and chill.

4. Stir the cream into the chilled custard, pour into a container, and freeze just until the ice cream is starting to harden. Whisk really well with a fork to disperse the ice crystals, then stir in the chocolate chips. Freeze until hard.

HOT FUDGE SUNDAE

The story goes that the name sundae is derived from the fact that these ice cream treats were originally served only on Sunday, the Sabbath, as they contained no soda water, a mix associated with alcohol.

SERVES 2

Choice of ice cream such as
    chocolate or vanilla fudge swirl
Whipped cream, to serve
Chocolate shavings, to decorate
FOR THE HOT FUDGE SAUCE
1 cup sugar
1 cup heavy or whipping cream
1/4 stick (2 tablespoons) butter,
    cut up
1 tablespoon corn syrup
4oz bittersweet chocolate, broken
    into pieces
1 teaspoon vanilla extract

1. To prepare the sauce, put the sugar, cream, butter, syrup, and chocolate in a heavy-based saucepan and set over a medium-high heat. Bring to a boil, stirring constantly, until the chocolate has melted and the mixture is smooth.

2. Reduce the heat to medium-low and cook for about 5 minutes, stirring frequently. Remove from the heat, stir in the vanilla extract, and keep warm.

3. Place 2 scoops ice cream in each of two scallop-edged sundae glasses or any dessert bowl. Spoon over 2 tablespoons fudge sauce and top with a swirl of whipped cream. Sprinkle with chocolate shavings and serve immediately.

CHOCOLATE & GINGER BOMBE

Another easy but impressive dessert. It can be made well in advance, as it will keep for up to one week well wrapped in the freezer.

SERVES 6–8

9oz bittersweet chocolate
   (50% cocoa solids),
   broken into pieces
4 knobs of stem ginger with syrup,
   finely chopped
2 cups heavy cream
5½oz meringues
Toasted flaked almonds, to serve
   (optional)

1. Line a 2¼lb pudding basin with plastic wrap.

2. Put the chocolate in a bowl and add 3 tablespoons stem ginger syrup and ½ cup cream. Melt over a pan of hot water or in the microwave for 1–2 minutes. Let cool slightly, then stir until smooth.

3. Add the chopped ginger to the chocolate and mix well.

4. Lightly whip the remaining cream until it is just holding its shape. Fold into the chocolate mixture.

5. Crush the meringues and fold into the chocolate mixture.

6. Spoon into the pudding basin, cover, and freeze for 3–4 hours until hard.

7. To serve, invert onto a serving plate and cut into wedges or slices. Sprinkle with toasted flaked almonds, if liked.

CHOCOLATE & ORANGE MOUSSE

This is a quick and easy dessert to knock up—a perfect end to a mid-week supper. Leave out the alcohol if serving to children.

SERVES 4

8oz good-quality bittersweet
    chocolate, broken into pieces
Grated rind and juice
    of 1 large orange
1 tablespoon Grand Marnier
4 eggs, separated
$\frac{1}{3}$ cup confectioner's sugar
$\frac{2}{3}$ cup heavy cream
Pared strips of orange rind,
    to decorate (optional)

1. Put the chocolate in a heatproof bowl. Add the orange rind and juice and the Grand Marnier and set over a saucepan of simmering water. Heat until the chocolate has melted, then stir until smooth. Let cool.

2. Whisk the egg yolks and confectioner's sugar together until the mixture becomes pale and frothy. Stir into the cooled chocolate mixture.

3. Lightly whip the cream and fold into the mousse mixture. Whisk the egg whites in a clean, grease-free bowl until soft peaks form and carefully fold into the mixture. Pour into four custard cups, individual ramekins, a soufflé dish, or a glass bowl and let chill for 3–4 hours until set. Decorate with orange rind, if liked.

CHOCOLATE GRANITA

Granita is an Italian ice—deliciously refreshing on a hot day. Bear in mind when making the granita that you need to stir the ice every hour for 4–5 hours to keep it from freezing solid.

SERVES 4

3½ cups water
1½ cups superfine sugar
½ cup unsweetened cocoa powder

1. Place all the ingredients in a saucepan and stirring continuously, bring to a boil. Stir until the sugar has dissolved, then take off the heat and let cool completely.

2. Pour into a large shallow container and freeze until ice crystals are starting to form around the edges. Stir the mixture around with a fork, bringing the ice crystals into the center.

3. Return to the freezer. Continue to do this every hour until the granita has set.

DOUBLE-CHOCOLATE MINI ALASKAS

These have a cookie base in place of the more usual cake base. Use the best-quality ice cream you can find, as it needs to freeze really firmly before being baked. Italian-style cooked meringue is more stable than the usual cold whipped method so it can withstand freezing and then high baking temperatures.

SERVES 4

5$\frac{1}{2}$oz bittersweet chocolate Graham crackers, crushed
$\frac{1}{2}$ stick (4 tablespoons) butter, melted
1$\frac{1}{2}$ cups good-quality chocolate chip ice cream
1 flaked chocolate bar, cut into 4
3 egg whites
$\frac{3}{4}$ cup superfine sugar
$\frac{1}{2}$ teaspoon vanilla extract
Unsweetened cocoa powder, for dusting

1. Mix the crushed cookies with the melted butter. Place an 3$\frac{1}{4}$in round cookie cutter on a greased baking sheet and spoon a quarter of the crumbs into it. Press down well, then remove the cutter. Repeat three times to make four bases.

2. Place the sheet in a freezer to firm up, about 30 minutes. Soften the ice cream slightly, then divide between the bases. Top each with a piece of flaked chocolate. Return to the freezer and leave until solid for 1–2 hours.

3. Whisk the egg whites, sugar, and vanilla extract until frothy. Place the bowl over a pan of gently simmering water and continue whisking until the meringue is thick and glossy, about 10 minutes. Remove from the heat and continue whisking until cool.

4. Take the bases out of the freezer and cover each completely with the meringue. Return to the freezer and freeze for at least 4 hours.

5. Preheat the oven to 425°F. Bake until golden for 6–8 minutes. Dust with the unsweetened cocoa powder before serving.

CHOCOLATE & CHERRY CHARLOTTE

You can of course make the chocolate cake and ice cream for this recipe but for a simple yet impressive throw-it-together dessert you can use shop-bought produce. Just make sure they are all the best quality you can afford.

SERVES 6

15oz can pitted black
   cherries in syrup
1lb 2oz best-quality bought
   plain chocolate cake
1 quart good-quality chocolate ice
   cream, softened just enough
   to be easy to scoop

1. Line a charlotte mold or 8in deep cake pan with plastic wrap. Drain the cherries reserving the syrup.

2. Cut the chocolate cake into fingers (about the same size as ladyfingers) and dip each piece into the reserved cherry syrup. Line the base and sides of the mold with the cake, leaving enough cake to cover the top.

3. Spoon half the softened ice cream into the base of the mold in an even layer. Cover with the drained cherries. Layer the remaining ice cream over and top with the reserved fingers of chocolate cake. Cover with plastic wrap and freeze for 2–3 hours until hard.

4. To serve, turn out the mold onto a serving plate and leave in the fridge for 15–20 minutes to soften slightly. Cut into wedges.

RICH MOCHA POTS

This dark, sultry take on chocolate mousse is a sophisticated, grown-up dessert. For best results use the finest chocolate you can find and chill the mousse well before serving.

SERVES 6–8

6oz bittersweet chocolate,
  broken into pieces
3 tablespoons strong black coffee
1 tablespoon butter
4 eggs, separated
2 tablespoons brandy
4 tablespoons confectioner's sugar
TO DECORATE
Whipped cream
grated chocolate or curls

1. Melt the chocolate in a bowl over a pan of hot water or in the microwave for 1–2 minutes. Stir in the coffee and butter until smooth.

2. Remove from the heat and whisk in the egg yolks one by one until the mixture is smooth and glossy. Whisk in the brandy, then set aside to cool and thicken slightly while you are whisking the egg whites.

3. Whisk the egg whites in a nonreactive bowl until stiff. Gradually add the sugar and continue whisking until glossy and thick. Fold into the cooled chocolate mixture.

4. Pour into six or eight small teacups or professional ramekins and chill for 3–4 hours until firm. Top with whipped cream and the grated chocolate or chocolate curls.

NOTE
Recipes using raw eggs should be avoided by infants, the elderly, pregnant women, and anyone with a compromised immune system.

CHOCOLATE PUDDING

This pudding was so popular in the 1950s, '60s, and '70s that packet mixes became available to make it at home. The pudding was literally child's play to make and everyone used the mixes, but it is just as easy to make an original from scratch.

SERVES 4–6

¾ cup sugar
¼ cup cornstarch
¼ teaspoon salt
¼ teaspoon ground cinnamon
   (optional)
1½ cups milk
½ cups whipping cream
½ stick (4 tablespoons) butter,
   cut into pieces
3½oz bittersweet chocolate, broken
   into pieces
1 egg
1 teaspoon vanilla extract
TO DECORATE
Whipped cream
Chocolate shavings

1. Stir together the sugar, cornstarch, salt, and cinnamon, if using, in a large heavy-based saucepan and gradually whisk in the milk and cream.

2. Add the cut-up butter and chopped chocolate and set over a medium heat. Cook until the chocolate melts and mixture thickens, whisking frequently. Bring to a boil and boil for 1 minute. Remove from the heat.

3. Beat the egg in a small bowl. Stir in a spoonful of the hot chocolate mixture, whisking constantly. Slowly pour the egg mixture into the chocolate, whisking constantly to prevent lumps from forming. The mixture will be very thick.

4. Strain the mixture into a large measuring jug pressing to push the it through. Stir in the vanilla extract.

5. Pour or spoon the pudding into dessert dishes or ramekins and let cool. Cover and chill for 2 hours or overnight. Serve decorated with whipped cream and a few chocolate shavings on top.

CHOCOLATE PROfiTEROLES

As a luxurious alternative to the classic profiterole, these miniature cream puffs are filled with chocolate cream.

MAKES **12 PROFITEROLES**

1 cup all-purpose flour

1 tablespoon confectioner's sugar

¾ cup water

¾ stick (6 tablespoons) butter, diced

3 eggs, beaten

1¼ heavy cream

2 tablespoons drinking
   chocolate powder

FOR THE SAUCE

4oz good-quality bittersweet
   chocolate, broken into pieces

2 tablespoons corn syrup

¼ stick (2 tablespoons) butter

4 tablespoons water

1. Preheat the oven to 400°F. Sift the flour and confectioner's sugar into a small bowl. Place the water and butter in a saucepan and heat gently until the butter has melted. Bring to a boil, then remove from the heat and quickly add the flour mixture, beating until smooth. Transfer to a bowl and let cool.

2. With a hand-held electric mixer, gradually beat the eggs into the mixture to make cream choux pastry. Fit a pastry bag with a plain tip and fill with the paste. Pipe 12 rounds onto a nonstick baking sheet. Bake until puffed and golden—about 18–20 minutes. Make a hole in the base of each profiterole and leave to cool on a wire rack.

3. Whip the cream with the chocolate powder until stiff. Fill a new piping bag with the chocolate cream and pipe carefully into the hole in the base of each individual profiterole.

4. To make the sauce, put the chocolate, syrup, butter, and water into a bowl and place over a pan of hot water or in the microwave for 1–2 minutes. Melt the chocolate and stir to mix. To serve, drizzle the warm chocolate sauce over the cream-filled profiteroles.

BLACK-BOTTOM CREAM PIE

SERVES 10–12

1 cup all-purpose flour

3 tablespoons unsweetened cocoa

2 tablespoons icing sugar

¾ stick (6 tablespoons) chilled
   butter, diced

1 egg yolk

1 tablespoon cold water

Grated chocolate, to decorate

FOR THE FILLING

4 egg yolks

¼ cup superfine sugar

4 teaspoons cornstarch

1⅔ cup milk

2oz bittersweet chocolate

1 tablespoon dark rum

FOR THE TOPPING

1½ teaspoons powdered gelatin

2 tablespoons cold water

½ cup heavy cream

2 tablespoons dark rum

3 egg whites

⅓ cup confectioner's sugar, sifted

½ teaspoon cream of tartar

1. Sift the flour, cocoa, and sugar into a bowl. Rub in the butter until the mixture resembles breadcrumbs. Mix the egg yolk and water, add to the dry ingredients, and mix to a firm dough. Knead, wrap, and chill for 30 minutes.

2. Put a baking sheet in the oven and preheat to 400°F. Sift a little extra flour and cocoa onto a surface, roll out the pastry, and line a greased 9in pie pan. Prick the base all over, line with foil and baking beans and bake for 15 minutes. Remove the foil and beans, and bake for 10 minutes more. Let cool.

3. For the filling, beat the egg yolks, sugar, and cornstarch together. Bring the milk to a boil, then pour over the egg mixture, beating. Return to the pan and stir over a low heat until thickened. Remove from the heat and stir in the chocolate until melted followed by the rum. Spoon the mixture into the pastry shell. Let cool.

4. For the topping, sprinkle the gelatin over the water in a bowl and let soak for 5 minutes. Set the bowl over a pan of barely simmering water and stir until dissolved. Let cool, but not set. Whip the cream until soft peaks form, then slowly beat in the gelatin and rum. Chill for 30 minutes or until starting to thicken, but not set.

5. Beat the egg whites until stiff. Beat in the confectioner's sugar, a tablespoon at a time, with the cream of tartar, then fold into the cream mixture. Spoon the mixture on top of the pie, chill until set, then decorate.

CHOCOLATE MARQUISE WITH VANILLA CRÈME ANGLAISE

A marquise is a super-rich, firm chocolate mousse—delicious!

SERVES 6–8

1lb bittersweet chocolate
   (70% cocoa solids),
   broken into pieces
$\frac{1}{4}$ cup very strong coffee
1 stick (8 tablespoons) butter
$\frac{1}{2}$ cup superfine sugar
4 egg yolks
$1\frac{2}{3}$ heavy cream
FOR THE CRÈME ANGLAISE
$1\frac{1}{4}$ cups milk
1 vanilla bean, split
4 egg yolks
$\frac{1}{2}$ cup superfine sugar

1. Line a $28\frac{1}{2}$ x $4\frac{1}{2}$ x $2\frac{1}{2}$in loaf pan or terrine dish with plastic wrap. Put the chocolate and coffee in a heatproof bowl over a pan of hot water or in the microwave for 1–2 minutes. Heat until the chocolate has melted. Stir and then leave to cool.

2. Beat the butter with $\frac{1}{4}$ cup of the sugar until pale and fluffy. In a separate bowl, whisk the egg yolks with the remaining sugar until thickened and pale. Lightly whip the cream until it just begins to hold its shape.

3. Beat the melted chocolate into the butter and fold in the egg yolk mixture, followed by the cream. Pour into the loaf pan and chill for 5–6 hours.

4. For the crème anglaise, bring the milk to a boil with the vanilla pod. Beat the egg yolks and sugar together. Add the hot milk, then return the mixture to the pan and stir over a low heat until it starts to thicken.

5. Remove the pan from the heat, leave the crème anglaise to cool, then scrape out the seeds from the vanilla bean and stir into the cold custard. Chill until ready to serve.

6. To serve, turn the mousse out onto a serving plate and serve with the vanilla crème anglaise.

WHITE CHOCOLATE PARFAIT

This heavenly little dessert may look innocent enough, but it will appeal to your most devilish instincts!

SERVES 4

6oz good-quality white chocolate,
    broken into pieces
2 tablespoons milk
1 vanilla beam
4 egg yolks
¾ cup confectioner's sugar
1¼ cup heavy cream
TO SERVE
Rich Chocolate Sauce or
    Easy Chocolate Sauce
    (see page 154) (optional)
Fresh cranberries (optional)

1. Melt the chocolate with the milk in a heatproof bowl over a pan of hot water or in the microwave for 1–2 minutes. Let cool.

2. Split the vanilla bean lengthwise and scrape out the seeds. Mix the seeds with the egg yolks and the confectioner's sugar and then whisk with a hand-held electric mixer until light and fluffy. Gently stir in the melted chocolate.

3. Lightly whip the cream and fold into the mixture. Divide the mousse between four custard cups, ramekins, or dariole molds and freeze for a minimum of 4 hours until firm.

4. To serve, briefly dip the base of the molds into warm water and invert on serving plates. Serve with a chocolate sauce and fresh berries such as cranberries, if liked.

KAHLÚA & CHOCOLATE TRIFLE

This variation on the classic tiramisù is very rich and totally addictive!

SERVES 4–6

½ cup strong fresh coffee
4 tablespoons Kahlúa
4oz ladyfingers
6 tablespoons superfine sugar
2 teaspoons vanilla extract
1lb mascarpone cheese
1 cup heavy cream
9oz bittersweet chocolate, grated
Unsweetened cocoa powder,
   for dusting

TIP
For a different flavor experience, use hazelnut liqueur instead of Kahlúa. Coffee and nut make an excellent combination.

1. Grease and line a 2¼lb loaf pan with plastic wrap. Mix the coffee and Kahlúa together. Dip the ladyfingers into the mixture and use a third of them to line the base of the pan.

2. Whisk the sugar and vanilla extract into the mascarpone with an hand-held electric mixer. Add the cream, a little at a time, whisking on a slow speed until smooth.

3. Spoon half of the mixture on top of the ladyfingers and spread evenly. Add half the grated chocolate, then repeat with a layer of the dipped fingers, the remaining cream mixture, grated chocolate, and a final layer of dipped sponge fingers. Drizzle any remaining coffee mixture over the top.

4. Cover with a layer of plastic wrap, then chill for 2–3 hours. Remove from the pan and peel off the plastic wrap. Dust with a generous amount of cocoa powder, slice, and serve.

WHITE & DARK CHOCOLATE CHEESECAKE

With a creamy soft texture and delicious chocolate flavor, these cute little cheesecakes will leave you begging for just one more!

SERVES 2

3oz Graham crackers, crushed

½ stick (4 tablespoons) butter, melted

1 tablespoon unsweetened cocoa powder

FOR THE FILLING

3oz white chocolate

3oz full-fat cream cheese

6 tablespoons crème fraîche or sour cream

2 tablespoons confectioner's sugar

TO DECORATE

3oz raspberries

1oz plain chocolate curls or grated bittersweet chocolate

1 tablespoon unsweetened cocoa powder

1. Mix together the cookie crumbs, butter, and cocoa. Use two 3¼in round cookie cutters to shape the base. Place the cutters on a flat plate and divide the crumb mixture between each of them. Press down on the crumbs until firmly packed.

2. Alternatively, you can line the base of two large ramekins with the crumb base. Place in the refrigerator to chill while you make the filling.

3. For the filling, melt the chocolate in a bowl over a pan of hot water or in the microwave for 1–2 minutes.

4. Beat together all the ingredients for the filling and pour on top of the bases. Chill for 2 hours or until firm.

5. Lift off the cookie cutters, top with raspberries, chocolate curls or the grated chocolate, and dust with cocoa.

CHOCOLATE & STRAWBERRY PAVLOVA

Chocolate and berries are a perfect combination and come together beautifully in this moreish meringue dessert.

SERVES 6–8

4 egg whites
Pinch of salt
1 cup superfine sugar
1 tablespoon cornstarch
2oz bittersweet chocolate,
   broken into pieces
Pinch of ground cinnamon
FOR THE FILLING
1¼ cup heavy cream
2oz milk chocolate, broken up
2 tablespoons milk
8oz strawberries, hulled and halved

1. Preheat the oven to 225°F. Draw an 7in circle on a piece of nonstick baking parchment and place ink-side down on a baking sheet.

2. Whisk the egg whites with the salt until stiff. Gradually whisk in the sugar and beat until very glossy and thick. Fold in the cornstarch, chopped chocolate, and cinnamon.

3. Spoon the meringue mixture into the middle and spread to the circle perimeter, hollowing out the middle slightly.

4. Cook for 1–1½ hours. Set aside to cool, then transfer the meringue to a serving plate.

5. For the filling, lightly whip the cream. Melt the chocolate with the milk over a gentle heat and let cool slightly. Roughly fold the chocolate into the cream, leaving it a little streaky. Pile the cream into the center of the pavlova and arrange the strawberries on top.

MISSISSIPPI MUD PIE

This is a classically rich dessert that will make a perfect end to any special meal.

SERVES 6–8

¾ stick (6 tablespoons) butter, softened

1 cup all-purpose flour

2 tablespoons iced water

¾ cup chopped walnuts

1 cup confectioner's sugar

8oz cream cheese, softened

2 cups heavy cream, whipped

6oz packet instant chocolate pudding mix

4 cups milk

1 heaping teaspoon unsweetened cocoa powder

TO DECORATE

Sifted unsweetened cocoa powder

Chopped nuts

1. Preheat the oven to 350°F.

2. Put the butter and flour in a mixing bowl and rub together lightly until the mixture resembles fine breadcrumbs. Stir in the water. Distribute the walnuts through the mixture, then press the mixture into a 9in pie dish. Bake for 12–15 minutes. Remove from the oven and let cool.

3. Combine the confectioner's sugar, cream cheese and 8oz of the whipped cream, reserving the rest for the topping in another bowl. Gently spread the mixture over the first cooked layer. Chill.

4. Prepare the pudding mix with the milk, according to the instructions on the packet, in a separate bowl. Mix in the cocoa powder.

5. Remove the chilled pie from the refrigerator and spread the chocolate pudding mix over the second layer. Top with the reserved whipped cream, dust with a fine layer of cocoa powder, and sprinkle with chopped nuts. Chill for a further 4 hours before serving.

DARK CHOCOLATE & TOFFEE TART

This dark and mysterious tart is quite rich so is best cut into small slices and served with some crème fraîche as an accompaniment.

SERVES 6–8

2½ cups all-purpose flour, plus extra for dusting

Pinch of salt

¼ cup confectioner's sugar

1½ sticks sweet butter, diced

2 egg yolks

4 tablespoons cold water

Unsweetened cocoa powder, for dusting

FOR THE FILLING

½ cup water

2 cups superfine sugar

4oz corn syrup

2½ sweet butter

1 cup heavy cream

1 teaspoon vanilla extract

4oz bittersweet chocolate (50% cocoa), grated

1. Sift the flour, salt, and confectioner's sugar into a mixing bowl. Add the butter and rub it in until the mixture resembles breadcrumbs.

2. Whisk the egg yolks with the cold water. Make a well in the center of the flour and pour in the egg mixture and mix together to form a dough. Knead briefly. Wrap in plastic wrap and leave to chill for 20 minutes.

3. Roll out the pastry on a lightly floured surface and use to line a 9½in loose-bottomed tart pan. Prick the pastry all over and chill for 10 minutes.

4. Preheat the oven to 375°F. Line the pastry case with waxed paper and fill with baking beans. Bake for 20 minutes or until golden and crisp. Remove the paper and beans and let cool.

5. For the filling, put the water in a large saucepan. Add the sugar and corn syrup and cook over a low heat until the sugar has dissolved. Increase the heat and let it bubble for about 10 minutes until the sauce is a deep caramel color.

6. Add half of the butter together with the cream and vanilla extract and stand back—it will bubble up. Stir until the mixture is smooth. Pour into the pastry case and chill for 2 hours until set and firm.

7. Melt the chocolate with the remaining butter in a heatproof bowl over a pan of hot water or in the microwave for 1–2 minutes. Let stand for 15 minutes.

8. Pour the chocolate mixture over the top of the tart, spreading it evenly with a spatula. Chill for at least 1 hour to set, then dust with cocoa powder.

SWEETHEARTS

A perfect dessert for Valentine's Day—or any day of the year that you want to show someone that you love them!

SERVES 2

4oz good-quality white chocolate
1 tablespoon corn syrup
1 tablespoon brandy
$^2/_3$ cups whipping cream
2 fresh strawberries, to decorate
FOR THE STRAWBERRY SAUCE
4oz strawberries, hulled
1 tablespoon confectioner's sugar

1. Break the chocolate into pieces and place in a heatproof bowl with the corn syrup and brandy. Sit the bowl over a pan of simmering water and allow to melt gently, stirring occasionally.

2. Remove the chocolate from the heat and let cool slightly. Whip the cream to soft peaks and carefully fold it into the chocolate mixture. Spoon into two $^1/_2$ cup heart-shaped molds and let set in the refridgerator for at least 2 hours.

3. To make the strawberry sauce, blitz the strawberries in a food processor or blender with the confectioner's sugar. Push through a strainer to remove the seeds.

4. Run the knife gently around the edge of each chocolate heart, then carefully turn out of the mold and transfer to a serving plate. Drizzle the strawberry sauce around the hearts and decorate with the strawberries.

CHOCOLATE CRÊPES WITH CARAMELIZED BANANAS & CREAM

When bananas are cooked they take on a much richer, smoother taste, and are a perfect accompaniment to these naughty chocolate crêpes.

MAKES **10 CRÊPES**

1¼ cups all-purpose flour
2 tablespoons unsweetened
   cocoa powder
2 tablespoons superfine sugar
2 eggs, beaten
¾ cup milk
½ cup water
1 tablespoon oil
FOR THE FILLING
4 bananas, sliced
⅓ cup confectioner's sugar
1¼ cups heavy cream, whipped

1. Mix the flour, cocoa powder, and superfine sugar together in a large bowl. Add the eggs and slowly pour in the milk and water, beating until you have a smooth batter. Stir in the oil, then let rest for 30 minutes.

2. Brush a large crêpe pan with a little oil and place over medium heat. Pour in a ladleful of batter and fry until set. Flip the crêpe over and quickly fry the other side. Set aside and keep warm. Repeat with the remaining batter.

3. For the filling, place the sliced bananas onto a nonstick baking sheet. Sprinkle with the confectioner's sugar and cook under a preheated grill for 3–4 minutes until golden. Fill each crêpe with a few banana slices and top with a spoonful of whipped cream. Fold the crêpes in half or quarters and serve immediately.

CHOCOLATE BRIOCHE PUDDING

This rich, indulgent pudding is surprisingly good eaten cold the day after baking. However, you may not be able to restrain yourself for that long!

SERVES 8

14oz brioche loaf
¾ stick (6 tablespoons) butter
7oz bittersweet chocolate
   (70% cocoa solids),
   broken into pieces
1¼ cups half-and-half cream
1¾ cups packet instant custard mix
1 cup milk

1. With a serrated bread knife, remove the crusts from the brioche, then cut into ½in slices. Grease a 9in square gratin dish (or 8 individual gratin dishes) with a little of the butter, then spread the remaining butter sparingly over the brioche. Lay half the slices in the bottom of the dish.

2. Sprinkle half the chocolate evenly over the brioche, then top with the remaining buttered slices. Bring the cream to a boil in a small saucepan, add the remaining chocolate, and stir until melted.

3. Whisk the custard and milk together, following the packet instructions, and stir in the chocolate cream. Pour the mixture over the brioche and let soak for 30 minutes.

4. Preheat the oven to 300°F. Place the gratin dish in a bain-marie (baking pan quarter-filled with water) and bake the pudding for 55–60 minutes until firm with a little wobble. Let stand for 5 minutes before serving.

CHOCOLATE CREAM PIE

A rich, dark chocolate filling is poured into a buttery pastry shell and chilled until set. Swirls of cream and curls of chocolate make this pie truly decadent.

SERVES 8–10

1½ cups all-purpose flour
2 tablespoons sugar
1 stick (8 tablespoons) butter, diced
1 egg yolk
2–3 teaspoons cold water
Chocolate curls, to decorate
FOR THE FILLING
½ cup cornstarch
⅓ cup superfine sugar
⅔ cup light cream
1 cup milk
3oz milk chocolate,
   broken into pieces
2 egg yolks
2 tablespoons butter
FOR THE TOPPING
1 cup heavy cream
½ teaspoon vanilla extract
2 teaspoons confectioner's sugar,
   sifted

1. Sift the flour and sugar into a bowl. Rub in the butter until the mixture resembles fine breadcrumbs.

2. Mix together the egg yolk and 2 teaspoons water and sprinkle over the dry ingredients. Mix to a firm dough, adding the extra water if needed. Lightly knead, then wrap in plastic wrap and chill for 30 minutes.

3. Put a baking sheet in the oven and preheat to 400°F. Roll out the pastry on a lightly floured surface and use to line a shallow 8–9in pie dish. Chill for 10 minutes.

4. Line the pie shell with baking parchment and baking beans. Bake blind for 15 minutes. Remove the parchment and beans and cook for another 8–10 minutes or until the pie shell is golden and crisp. Remove from the oven and let cool on a wire rack.

5. To make the filling, mix the cornstarch and sugar in a nonstick pan. Gradually blend in the cream and then stir in the milk and chocolate. Gently heat, stirring constantly until the chocolate melts and the mixture thickens and boils. Remove from the heat.

CHOCOLATE TIP

To make thick chocolate curls, melt 6oz milk chocolate with 2 tablespoons pure white vegetable fat, stirring until smooth. Pour into a small pan lined with baking parchment, to produce a thick block. Chill until set. Let the block come to room temperature. Hold the block over a plate and pull the blade of a swivel-bladed peeler firmly along the edge.

6. Beat the egg yolks in a small bowl. Stir in a few spoonfuls of the chocolate mixture, one at a time, then pour the egg mixture back into the chocolate mixture in the pan, stirring constantly. Cook and continue to stir for another 1 minute but do not boil.

7. Remove from the heat and stir in the butter. Cool for a few minutes, then pour into the pie shell. To prevent a skin forming, press a circle of dampened baking parchment onto the surface of the filling. Let cool, then chill for 2 hours. Remove the baking parchment.

8. For the topping, pour the cream into a chilled bowl. Stir in the vanilla extract and sugar. Whip until the cream forms soft peaks, then spoon into a pastry bag with a large star nozzle and pipe a lattice pattern on top of the pie. Scatter with chocolate curls and serve.

CHOCOLATE PECAN PIE

The pie is filled with a deliciously fudgy mixture of nuts, chocolate, and maple syrup. Delicious warm or cold with a dollop of whipped cream.

SERVES 8–10

2 cups all-purpose flour

Pinch of salt

4 tablespoons confectioner's sugar, plus extra for dusting (optional)

1 stick (8 tablespoons) sweet butter, diced

2–3 tablespoons cold water

Whipped cream, to serve

FOR THE FILLING

1½ cups pecans

5oz bittersweet chocolate, roughly chopped

½ stick (4 tablespoons) sweet butter, diced

3 eggs

1 cup light brown sugar

¾ cup maple syrup

1 tablespoon all-purpose flour

1. Sift the flour into a mixing bowl with the salt and confectioner's sugar. Add the butter and using your fingertips, rub the butter into the flour until the mixture resembles coarse breadcrumbs.

2. Add cold water and using your hands, a narrow spatula, or a palette knife start to bring the dough together, adding a little more water, if it is necessary.

3. Turn the dough onto a lightly floured surface and knead briefly, just until the dough is smooth. Form into a neat ball, flatten into a disc, and wrap in plastic wrap. Chill for at least 20 minutes.

4. Remove the pastry from the refrigerator and leave at room temperature for 5–10 minutes. Unwrap and place on a lightly floured surface. Lightly flour the top of the dough and a rolling pin and roll out the pastry to line a 10-in loose-bottomed tart pan. Prick the base and chill for 10 minutes.

5. Line the pastry shell with baking parchment and weigh down with baking beans. Bake in a preheated oven at 350°F until golden and crisp—about 20 minutes. Remove the paper and beans.

6. Reduce the oven to 325°F. Roughly chop three-quarters of the pecans with a large knife and scatter over the cooked pastry case.

7. Melt the chocolate and butter in a bowl set over a pan of hot water or in the microwave for 1–2 minutes. Stir and let cool.

8. Whisk together the eggs, brown sugar, and maple syrup. Stir in the cooled chocolate and fold in the flour. Pour into the pastry case. Arrange the remaining nuts on top and bake until the center is just set—about 50–55 minutes.

9. Remove the pie from the oven and let cool slightly. Dust with confectioner's sugar, if liked, and serve with whipped cream. If made ahead, reheat in a 300°F oven for 5–10 minutes.

THE CHOCOLATERIE

CHOCOLATE TRUFFLES WITH ORANGE FLOWER WATER

For dark chocolate truffles, replace the white chocolate with bittersweet and use brandy instead of the orange flower water.

MAKES 10 TRUFFLES

⅓ cup heavy cream
5½oz white chocolate, broken into pieces
1–2 tablespoons orange flower water
4 tablespoons unsweetened cocoa powder

1. Heat the cream in a small saucepan until almost boiling. Take off the heat and let cool for 5 minutes or until warm enough to touch.

2. Stir in the chocolate and orange flower water and mix until smooth.

3. Dust your hands in a little cocoa and put the remainder on a flat plate. Scoop out a walnut-sized piece of chocolate with a spoon and roll it in your hands. Roll in cocoa and put on a clean plate. Repeat with the remaining mixture.

4. Chill for 1 hour to firm up before serving.

SIMPLE CHOCOLATE FUDGE

This is a great recipe for getting the kids involved, as apart from melting the chocolate and butter, it requires no other cooking.

MAKES ABOUT 25 SQUARES

½ stick (4 tablespoons) sweet butter
4oz bittersweet chocolate
    (70% cocoa solids),
    broken into pieces
2½ cups confectioner's sugar, sifted

1. Line a 7in square cake pan with nonstick baking parchment.

2. Melt the butter and chocolate in a bowl over hot water or in the microwave for 1–2 minutes. Let cool for a couple of minutes, then stir until smooth.

3. Beat half the confectioner's sugar into the melted chocolate and butter and stir in a tablespoon of boiling water. Repeat with the remaining confectioner's sugar and a further tablespoon of boiling water.

4. Spoon the fudge into the pan, level out the surface, and refrigerate until hard. Cut into small squares.

TIP
As a delicious variation, add a handful of raisins or chopped nuts to the mixture before you pour it into the pan.

SMOOTH CHOCOLATE & DRIED CRANBERRY FUDGE

It is easiest to make good fudge with a sugar thermometer, but the soft–ball test works well if you are vigilant and test every minute or so. If you can't find dried cranberries you could substitute raisins.

MAKES ABOUT 25 SQUARES

1¼ cups full-fat milk
2 cups sugar
2oz bittersweet chocolate (70% cocoa solids), broken into pieces
¼ stick (2 tablespoons) sweet butter
½ cup dried cranberries

1. Line a 7in square cake pan with nonstick baking parchment.

2. Heat the milk and sugar in a large, heavy-bottomed saucepan, stirring until the sugar has dissolved.

3. Add the chocolate and butter and stir until smooth. Continue to cook, stirring to prevent the mixture burning, until the temperature reaches 239°F. Test the mixture by dropping a tiny bit into a bowl of cold water. If it holds its shape and can be rolled into a soft ball it is ready.

4. Take the saucepan off the heat, add the cranberries, and start to beat, for about 4–5 minutes until really thick. Immediately pour into the prepared pan and let cool completely. Cut into squares to serve.

CHOCOLATE TOFFEE

A sticky toothsome treat! Successful toffee making is all about the sugar reaching the correct temperature. The easiest way to guarantee success is to use a sugar thermometer.

MAKES ABOUT 36 PIECES

2 cups turbinado sugar
2¼ sticks sweet butter
¾ cup corn syrup
1oz unsweetened cocoa powder

1. Line a 8 x 8in square cake pan with non-stick baking parchment.

2. Place all the ingredients in a large, heavy-based saucepan and cook slowly, stirring, until the sugar has dissolved.

3. Turn the heat up and bring to a boil until the temperature reaches hard ball stage (248°F) on a sugar thermometer. If you don't have a thermometer drop a little bit of the mixture into a bowl of cold water and if it hardens immediately it is ready.

4. Pour the mixture into the prepared pan and leave until cold and hard. Cut into pieces.

TIP
Don't be afraid to keep testing the toffee with your sugar thermometer to make sure you reach hard-ball stage.

MILK CHOCOLATE & PINE NUT CLUSTERS

Making the caramel is a bit of a fiddle but worth the effort when you bite into the fudgy, nutty center. Try and get the best milk chocolate—it really makes a difference.

MAKES ABOUT 25 CLUSTERS

¾ cup superfine caster sugar
½ cup heavy cream
2 cups pine nuts
7oz good-quality milk chocolate,
    broken into pieces

1. Line a baking sheet with nonstick baking parchment.

2. Place the sugar in a wide saucepan and heat slowly without stirring. Let the sugar melt without coloring too much. It should be a golden caramel color.

3. Pour in the cream, being careful as it bubbles up. Stir over a low heat until the caramel is smooth. Take off the heat and stir in the pine nuts. Pour onto the prepared baking sheet and let get cool completely.

4. Once the mixture has cooled take spoonfuls, and with slightly damp hands, roll into balls. Set aside.

5. Melt the chocolate in a bowl over a pan of hot water or in the microwave for 1–2 minutes. Cool a little. Place a clean sheet of nonstick baking parchment on a board.

6. It is messy but it is easiest to dip the caramel nut clusters into the melted chocolate with your fingers. Place them on the lined board and let harden. Serve in petit four cases or simply on a serving dish.

ROCKY ROAD FUDGE

The melted marshmallows give the fudge a creamy texture.

MAKES ABOUT 25 SQUARES

1¾ cups milk
2⅓ cups sugar
½ stick (4 tablespoons) sweet butter
1oz unsweetened cocoa powder
3oz marshmallows

1. Line a small square cake pan, about 6 x 6in, with nonstick baking parchment.

2. In a large, heavy-bottomed saucepan heat the milk and sugar and stir until the sugar has dissolved. Add the butter and cocoa powder and bring to a boil, still stirring.

3. Continue to cook, stirring to prevent the mixture burning, until the temperature reaches 239°F. Test the mixture by dropping a tiny bit into a bowl of cold water. If it holds its shape and can be rolled into a soft ball it is ready.

4. Take the saucepan off the heat and stir in the marshmallows. Beat until the mixture is thick and has lost its gloss.

5. Pour into the prepared pan and let cool and harden. Cut into squares to serve.

MINI CHOCOLATE & RAISIN LOGS

If you want to make these at Christmas you could run the prongs of a fork across the tops of the logs and make little holly like leaves and berries with colored marzipan.

MAKES ABOUT 15 LOGS

5oz bittersweet chocolate
   (70% cocoa solids),
   broken into pieces
1 stick (8 tablespoons) sweet butter,
   cut into small pieces
½ cup confectioner's sugar, sifted
2 egg yolks
¾ cup raisins
Unsweetened cocoa powder, for
   rolling and dusting
Confectioner's sugar, for dusting

1. Melt the chocolate in a bowl over a pan of hot water or in the microwave for 1–2 minutes. Cool a little, then stir in the pieces of butter, little by little until smooth.

2. Stir in the confectioner's sugar, egg yolks and finally the raisins. Place the mixture in the refrigerator to harden up.

3. Dust a work surface with cocoa powder and roll spoonfuls of the chocolate mixture into little logs. Dust with a little more cocoa powder and a sprinkling of confectioner's sugar before serving.

CHOCOLATE & PEANUT BRITTLE

You really need a sugar thermometer to make brittle, so don't attempt this without one. I coat the brittle in a mixture of bittersweet and milk chocolate, but you could use all bittersweet or all milk chocolate if you have a favorite.

MAKES ABOUT 500G

³/₄ cup superfine sugar
1 cup corn syrup
1¹/₂ cups unsalted peanuts
¹/₄ stick (2 tablespoons) sweet butter
1 teaspoon baking soda
3¹/₂oz bittersweet chocolate (70% cocoa solids), broken into pieces
3¹/₂oz milk chocolate, broken into pieces

1. Grease a 10 x 14in jelly roll pan.

2. Place the sugar and corn syrup in a large, heavy-based saucepan and bring to a boil, stirring.

3. When the temperature has reached 284°F, add the peanuts and butter and continue to cook until the temperature reaches 305°F. Take off the heat and add the baking soda.

4. Pour into the prepared pan and leave until cold and hard. Break into pieces.

5. Melt the chocolate in a bowl over a pan of hot water or in the microwave for 1–2 minutes. Let cool a little, then stir to combine.

6. Dip the ends of the brittle pieces into the melted chocolate, then let harden on a sheet of nonstick baking parchment.

BITTER CARAMEL & CHOCOLATE ROCKS

The hint of dark brown sugar gives these candies a sophisticated flavor. Watch the almonds carefully when you are grilling them —they burn very easily.

MAKES ABOUT 15 ROCKS

1¾ cups blanched whole almonds
¼ cup dark brown sugar
7oz bittersweet chocolate
  (70% cocoa solids),
  broken into pieces
1 tablespoon vegetable oil

1. Preheat the broiler to its hottest setting. Place the almonds in a food processor or blender and pulse two or three times until the nuts are roughly broken up. Turn onto a nonstick baking sheet, sprinkle the nuts with the sugar, and mix well.

2. Cook them under the grill for 3–4 minutes turning them over frequently to ensure even color. Remove and let cool.

3. Melt the chocolate and oil in a bowl over a pan of hot water or in the microwave for 1–2 minutes. Let cool a little, then stir until smooth. Stir in the cooled nuts.

4. Either spoon into petit four cases or leave until the mixture has hardened a little and spoon onto nonstick baking parchment. Leave until completely hard.

MILK CHOCOLATE & PISTACHIO TORRONE

Torrone is an Italian nougat full of nuts and candied fruit. It is best not attempted without a sugar thermometer.

MAKES ABOUT 50–60 PIECES

2⅓ cups sugar
1 cup honey
3 egg whites
2 cups shelled, unsalted pistachios
2oz candied orange peel,
    finely chopped
7oz milk chocolate,
    broken into pieces

1. Line a baking pan, about 9 x 13in with nonstick baking parchment.

2. Place the sugar and honey in a heavy-based saucepan and slowly bring to a boil, stirring occasionally.

3. Place the thermometer in the liquid and when the temperature is coming up to 284°F, start to whisk the egg whites until stiff. When the temperature of the liquid reaches 320°F (hard crack), take off the heat and pour onto the whisked egg whites, continuing to whisk until the mixture starts to get really tacky and harden around the whisk, about 3–4 minutes. Stir in the nuts and orange peel, then spoon into the prepared pan.

4. Dampen your hands with water and pat down the torrone to the edges of the pan. Cover with a layer of nonstick baking parchment and leave to get cold and hard.

5. Melt the chocolate in a bowl over a pan of hot water or in the microwave for 1–2 minutes. Let cool for a minute or two, pour over the torrone, and spread to the edges with a spatula. Let harden and then cut into squares.

WHITE CHOCOLATE & PRALINE HEARTS

These are great fun to do for Valentine's Day. See the Chocolate Praline Torte recipe (see page 58) for instructions on how to make praline.

MAKES ABOUT 12 HEARTS

7oz white chocolate,
  broken into pieces
1 tablespoon sweet butter
¼ cup crushed praline (see page 58)

1. Place a sheet of nonstick baking parchment on a flat board. Trace around a heart-shaped cookie cutter (about 2–3in). You should have about 12 cookies.

2. Melt the chocolate and the butter in a bowl over hot water or in the microwave for 1–2 minutes. Let cool a little, then stir until smooth.

3. Following the shape of the heart spread out spoonfuls of the chocolate. Then leaving a little margin around the edges sprinkle over the praline and press down gently so it sticks into the chocolate.

4. Refrigerate until hard, then peel off the paper. Serve with coffee as an after-dinner sweetie.

TIP
For variety, try making these with bittersweet chocolate or a combination of white and bittersweet chocolate. Proceed as described above.

RICH CHOCOLATE & COFFEE SQUARES

Serve as bite-size treats for after dinner or at a wedding. You could cover them with a coating of glacé icing (see page 154), but I happen to like them plain.

MAKES ABOUT 30 SQUARES

5oz bittersweet chocolate
   (70% cocoa solids),
   broken into pieces
1¼ sticks (10 tablespoons)
   sweet butter
2 teaspoons instant coffee
   granules dissolved in
   2 tablespoons boiling water
2 eggs, separated
½ cup superfine sugar
½ cup ground almonds
⅓ all-purpose flour

1. Preheat the oven to 350°F. Grease and baseline a 7½ x 7½in square cake pan with nonstick baking parchment.

2. Melt the chocolate and butter in a bowl over a pan of hot water or in the microwave for 1–2 minutes. Let cool a little, then stir in the coffee. Set aside.

3. Whisk together the egg yolks and sugar until pale and thick. Stir in the cooled chocolate mixture followed by the ground almonds and flour.

4. Whisk the egg whites to soft peaks, then fold into the chocolate. Pour the mixture into the prepared pan and bake for 15 minutes or until just firm to the touch.

5. Let cool in the pan, then turn out and cut into small squares.

MINI CHOCOLATE MOUSSE & STRAWBERRY TARTS

MAKES 24 TARTS

FOR THE PASTRY

1⅓ cups all-purpose flour

1 tablespoon unsweetened
    cocoa powder

⅓ cup confectioner's sugar, sifted

1¼ sticks (10 tablespoons) sweet
    butter, cut into cubes

1 egg, beaten

FOR THE MOUSSE

6oz bittersweet chocolate
    (50% cocoa solids),
    broken into pieces

3 eggs, separated

3–4 small strawberries, finely sliced,
    to decorate

1. Preheat the oven to 350°F.

2. To make the pastry, mix together the flour, cocoa powder, and confectioner's sugar in a bowl. Add the butter and rub in until the mixture resembles fine breadcrumbs. Stir in the egg and enough cold water to bring the mixture together.

3. Roll out the dough thinly on a floured surface and stamp out rounds big enough to line 2 12-cup mini tart trays. Prick the bases and chill for 30 minutes.

4. Bake in the oven for 10 minutes until the pastry is cooked. When they have cooled a little remove the pastry cups from the trays and cool on a wire rack.

5. To make the mousse, melt the chocolate in a bowl over a pan of hot water or in the microwave for 1–2 minutes. Cool a little, then stir in the egg yolks. Whisk the egg whites until stiff and fold into the chocolate mixture.

6. When the tarts are cold spoon or pipe the mousse into the tarts and leave in a cool place to set. Serve decorated with slices of strawberry.

CHOCOLATE DIPPED FRUIT

As an alternative dessert put the bowls of freshly prepared fruit on the table and let each person dip their choice of fruit into the melted chocolate. If you are serving it this way, stir 1–2 tablespoons heavy cream into the melted chocolate beforehand to prevent the chocolate going hard again.

SERVES 4

3½oz chocolate of your choice (a mixture of plain and milk is delicious)

8–10½oz mixed fruit such as strawberries, cherries, cape gooseberries, grapes, bananas, pears, ready-to-eat dried figs, dates, or apricots

1. Line a baking sheet with nonstick baking parchment.

2. Melt the chocolate in a bowl over a pan of hot water or in the microwave for 1–2 minutes.

3. With a skewer or toothpick quickly dip the pieces of fruit into the chocolate, allowing the excess to drip off, and place them on the lined baking sheet. Let cool.

TIP
This can be prepared a few hours in advance but no longer, as the fresh fruit will start to go soggy and discolor.

CHOCOLATE PEPPERMINT FONDANTS

These are easy fondants that you can make with the children. Try and find authentic peppermint essence and not peppermint flavoring, which can have a very harsh taste.

MAKES ABOUT 25 FONDANTS

3½ confectioner's sugar, sifted, plus extra for rolling out
1 egg white
A few drops of peppermint essence
3½oz bittersweet chocolate (70% cocoa solids), broken into pieces
1 tablespoon vegetable oil

1. Place the sifted confectioner's sugar in a large mixing bowl and work in the egg white, adding a little water to make a smooth paste. Add a few drops of peppermint essence—enough to suit your tastes.

2. Liberally dust a work surface with confectioner's sugar and roll out the paste to a thickness of about ½in. Stamp out 1in rounds with a cookie cutter.

3. Place the discs on a wire rack and let dry out for about 12 hours.

4. Melt the chocolate and oil in a bowl over a pan of hot water or in the microwave for 1–2 minutes. Leave for a minute or two to cool and then stir until smooth.

5. Dip the peppermint discs into the chocolate and place on a piece of nonstick baking parchment to harden.

FRENCH COLETTES

Lining the petit four cases with the melted chocolate is a bit fiddly, but the end results are pretty impressive.

MAKES 16 COLETTES

7oz plain chocolate
(70% cocoa solids),
broken into pieces
½ stick (4 tablespoons) sweet butter
½ cup heavy cream

1. Melt 4oz chocolate in a bowl over a pan of hot water or in the microwave for 1–2 minutes. Let cool a little, then stir until smooth.

2. Take 16 petit four cases and, one by one, spoon a little chocolate into the bottom. Tip the case around making sure the sides of the case are covered with chocolate. Pour off any excess into the bowl. Place in the refrigerator to harden up. Repeat with the remaining cases.

3. Repeat the whole process a second time. Check the chocolate case is thick enough by peeling off one of the petit four cases. If the chocolate is not thick enough repeat a third time. When the cases have hardened up peel off the paper and refrigerate while you make the filling.

4. Melt the remaining chocolate in a bowl over a pan of hot water or in the microwave for 1–2 minutes. Cool for a minute, then beat in the butter a little at a time until the mixture is smooth. Lightly whip the cream and fold into the chocolate.

5. Let the chocolate filling set slightly (about 5 minutes in the refrigerator), then spoon into a pastry bag and pipe into the chocolate cases or spoon the filling directly into the cases, levelling out the top. Leave in the refrigerator to set.

CHOCOLATE PRALINES

These little pralines are light and melting. Unlike European pralines that contain nuts, these are the American versions, which are nut-free.

MAKES ABOUT 25 PRALINES

¾ cup sugar

⅔ cup light brown sugar

⅔ cup heavy cream

½ stick (4 tablespoons) sweet butter

3oz plain chocolate
   (70% cocoa solids),
   broken into pieces

1. Line a baking sheet with nonstick baking parchment.

2. Place the sugars and cream in a large, heavy-based saucepan and, stirring slowly, bring to a boil. When the mixture reaches soft-ball stage (244°F) take it off the heat and beat in the butter and chocolate.

3. Working quickly drop spoonfuls of the mixture onto the baking parchment. If the mixture becomes too solid add a touch of boiling water. Let cool completely.

TIP

As a variation and for a contrast of flavors, drizzle the pralines with melted bittersweet chocolate.

FROZEN ICE CREAM TRUFFLES

You really must buy the best-quality ice cream for these truffles as cheap, soft-scoop ice cream won't hold its shape.

MAKES 12 TRUFFLES

1 small tub best-quality
  ice cream, vanilla or coffee
4oz bittersweet chocolate
  (70% cocoa solids),
  broken into pieces
1 teaspoon vegetable oil

1. Working quickly, with a melon baller scoop out 12 balls of ice cream and place on a sheet of baking parchment. Immediately place in the freezer for at least 1 hour.

2. Melt the chocolate in a bowl over a pan of hot water or in the microwave for 1–2 minutes. Let cool a little, then stir in the oil.

3. Very quickly dip each ice cream ball into the melted chocolate and replace in the freezer immediately to harden up. Serve with toothpicks as an after-dinner treat.

MINI CHOCOLATE, CARAMEL & COCONUT SQUARES

MAKES ABOUT 36 SQUARES

FOR THE BASE

9oz graham crackers biscuits
  or similar
$\frac{1}{2}$ stick (4 tablespoons) sweet butter,
  melted

FOR THE CARAMEL

12oz sweetened condensed milk
1 cup shredded coconut
$\frac{1}{2}$ cup light brown sugar
$\frac{1}{2}$ stick (4 tablespoons) sweet butter
200g plain chocolate
  (50–70% cocoa solids),
  broken into pieces
2 tablespoons vegetable oil

1. Preheat the oven to 350°F. Base-line a $7\frac{1}{2}$ x $7\frac{1}{2}$in square cake pan with nonstick baking parchment.

2. Finely crush the biscuits and stir in the melted butter. Press into the base of the prepared pan and bake in the oven for 5 minutes. Cool slightly.

3. To make the caramel, place the condensed milk, coconut, sugar, and butter in a saucepan and stir over a low heat for 8–10 minutes until thick. Spread the caramel over the biscuit base and cook in the oven for 5–10 minutes. Let cool completely.

4. Melt the chocolate in a bowl over a pan of hot water or in the microwave for 1–2 minutes. Let cool a little, then stir in the oil. Pour over the caramel, spreading the chocolate to the edges. Leave until hard, then cut into little squares.

MARBLED CHOCOLATE EGG

MAKES 1 EGG

8oz best-quality bittersweet
   chocolate, broken into pieces
4oz best-quality white chocolate,
   broken into pieces
1oz melted chocolate to join edges

1. First you need to polish the inside of a 6in plastic egg mold with a soft cloth. This will help when you come to unmold the chocolate later.

2. Place the chocolates in two separate bowls and melt over pans of hot water or in the microwave for 1–2 minutes. Let cool slightly.

3. Drop alternate spoonfuls into each half, tilting the molds so the chocolates run together and coat the inside of the molds. Don't put too much chocolate into the molds—you are going to do at least two layers anyway. Then draw through the chocolate with a skewer so you get a marbled effect. Refrigerate until set.

4. Repeat with a second layer, refrigerate, then repeat again. Refrigerate until the chocolate is completely set.

5. Carefully pull each mold from the chocolate, you may need to ease it out with the point of a knife.

6. To join together the two sides, spread a little bit of the melted chocolate along the edges and press together. Place in the refrigerator until hard.

THE TOPPINGS

EASY CHOCOLATE SAUCE

This sauce is perfect as a storecupboard standby as it takes next to no time to rustle up and complements a multitude of desserts.

SERVES 4

½ cup unsweetened cocoa powder
½ cup superfine sugar
1½ cups water
¼ stick (2 tablespoons) unsalted
    butter

1. Place all the ingredients in a saucepan and, stirring gently, bring to a boil.
2. Let the sauce boil for 2 minutes, without stirring, then let cool a few minutes before serving.

RICH BITTERSWEET CHOCOLATE SAUCE

A very indulgent sauce that can be served hot or cold.

SERVES 4

8oz bittersweet chocolate
    (70% cocoa solids),
    broken into pieces
¾ stick (6 tablespoons) sweet butter
¾ cup heavy cream

1. Place all the ingredients in a saucepan and stir over a gentle heat until the sauce is smooth and glossy.

WHITE CHOCOLATE FUDGE SAUCE

This can be poured over a bittersweet chocolate sponge as a wonderful contrast. Alternatively, it can double up as a white chocolate fondue—dip in a selection of fresh fruit or pieces of Madeira cake. It is also delicious served drizzled over a fresh fruit salad.

SERVES 6

8oz white chocolate,
   broken into pieces
1 cup milk
1 cup heavy cream
1 teaspoon vanilla extract
3 teaspoons cornstarch mixed
   with 1 tablespoon milk

1. Place the chocolate, milk, cream, and vanilla extract in a saucepan and stir over a gentle heat until the chocolate has melted.

2. Stir in the cornstarch mixture and cook, stirring for 1–2 minutes until the sauce is thick enough to coat the back of a wooden spoon. Serve warm.

STICKY CHOCOLATE FUDGE SAUCE

This sauce is possibly the most popular sauce and one of the easiest to make with all the ingredients going into the pan at the same time.

SERVES 4–6

8oz bittersweet chocolate
   (50–70% cocoa solids),
   broken into pieces
$\frac{2}{3}$ cup light brown sugar
1 cup heavy cream
$\frac{1}{4}$ stick (2 tablespoons) sweet butter
1 tablespoon corn syrup

1. Place all the ingredients in a saucepan and stir over a gentle heat until the sauce is smooth. Serve hot.

TIP
For a slightly different flavor try this delicious sauce using maple syrup instead of corn syrup.

CHOCOLATE CUSTARD SAUCE

The perfect accompaniment to a steamed chocolate pudding.

SERVES 4–6

9oz light brown sugar
¾ cup unsweetened cocoa powder
1 tablespoon cornstarch
1½ cups milk
1 tablespoon sweet butter

1. Place the sugar and cocoa powder in a saucepan. In a bowl mix the cornstarch with a little of the milk, then pour in the rest of the milk. Pour this into the saucepan.

2. Stir over a gentle heat until the sauce thickens, then whisk in the butter. Serve warm.

EASY CHOCOLATE BUTTERCREAM FROSTING

Perfect for filling children's fairy cakes.

MAKES ENOUGH TO FILL AND COAT A 7–8IN CAKE

2 tablespoons unsweetened cocoa powder, sifted

1½ sticks sweet butter, softened

2 cups confectioner's sugar, sifted

1. Mix the cocoa powder with a little boiling water to make a smooth paste.

2. Beat the butter until soft and add the cocoa powder. Gradually beat in the confectioner's sugar.

GLACÉ ICING

This icing is suitable for covering cakes and pastries rather than filling them. It will give a glossy finish to your cake.

MAKES ENOUGH TO COAT A 7–8IN CAKE

1 cup confectioner's sugar, sifted
1 tablespoon unsweetened cocoa powder, sifted

1. Mix together the confectioner's sugar and cocoa powder. Stir in a tablespoon of boiling water and mix until smooth. You may need to add a touch more water to get the right consistency.

2. This icing needs to be used straight away or it forms a crust.

GANACHE FROSTING

A lovely, rich and decadent topping to any dessert.

MAKES ENOUGH TO FILL AND COVER A 7–8IN CAKE

10oz plain chocolate (50–70% cocoa solids), broken into pieces
¾ cup heavy cream
¼ stick (2 tablespoons) sweet butter, cut into small pieces

1. Place the chocolate and heavy cream in a saucepan and stir over a gentle heat until the chocolate has melted.

2. Stir in the butter. Let cool until the mixture has a spreadable consistency.

SOUR CREAM & CHOCOLATE FROSTING

The sour cream in this frosting cuts through the sweetness of the chocolate to lighten it slightly.

MAKES ENOUGH TO FILL AND COAT A 7–8IN CAKE

7oz bittersweet chocolate
(50% cocoa solids),
broken into pieces
½ stick (4 tablespoons) sweet butter
1⅔ cups sour cream or crème fraîche
1 cup confectioner's sugar, sifted

1. Melt the chocolate and butter in a bowl over a pan of hot water or in the microwave for 1–2 minutes. Let cool for a few minutes, then stir until smooth.

2. Stir in the sour cream followed by the confectioner's sugar. Chill until you have a firm enough consistency to frost a cake.

CHOCOLATE TIP

To make marble-effect shards of chocolate, melt equal quantities of bittersweet and white chocolate. Spread the bittersweet chocolate onto a tray lined with nonstick baking parchment so a few millimeters thick. Drizzle over the white chocolate. Gently drag it through, making a pattern of your choice. Cool then break up to use as decoration.

CHOCOLATE FUDGE FROSTING

A perfect fudgy topping to any cake – the grainy texture of the frosting provides an especially delightful contrast to a soft sponge.

MAKES ENOUGH TO FILL AND COAT A 7–8IN CAKE

6oz bittersweet chocolate
   (50% cocoa solids),
   broken into pieces
1³/₄ sticks sweet butter
¹/₃ cup light brown sugar
2 tablespoons heavy cream
2¹/₄ cups confectioner's sugar, sifted

1. Melt the chocolate in a bowl over a pan of hot water or in the microwave for 1–2 minutes. Let cool slightly.

2. Place the butter, sugar, and cream in a saucepan and stir over a gentle heat until the sugar has dissolved. Stir in the melted chocolate and finally beat in the confectioner's sugar. The mixture will begin to separate. When it does add 3–4 tablespoons boiling water and beat until glossy and smooth.

THE BAR

HOT CHOCOLATE WITH CARDAMOM

If you're in need of a comforting drink, this is the one for you. Warmed milk has been used as the classic bedtime soporific for centuries, and the soothing taste of chocolate and sweetly spiced cardamom are just delicious.

MAKES 2

2 cups full-fat milk
4 cardamom pods, bruised
4oz bittersweet chocolate,
    broken into pieces
½ cup heavy cream
Unsweetened cocoa powder or
    shaved chocolate, to decorate
    (optional)

1. Pour the milk into a pan and add the cardamom pods. Bring almost to a boil, then remove from the heat and let steep for 10 minutes.

2. Remove the cardamom pods and return the pan to the heat. Heat gently, until almost boiling, and then whisk in the chocolate until melted. Pour into two large cups or mugs.

3. Whip the cream until it stands in very soft peaks and spoon on top of the hot chocolate. Decorate with cocoa powder or shaved chocolate, if you like.

MEXICAN HOT CHOCOLATE

Mexican chocolate is a mixture of chocolate, ground almonds, and spices, sweetened with sugar, and you can buy it in specialist stores. Here you can make your own deliciously aromatic drink.

MAKES 2

2¼ cups full-fat milk
½ cup ground almonds
¼ cup superfine sugar
2 teaspoons ground cinnamon
1 vanilla bean, split down the center
3½oz bittersweet chocolate
(50–70% cocoa solids),
broken into pieces

1. Place the milk, ground almonds, sugar, cinnamon, and vanilla bean in a saucepan and bring to a boil over a gentle heat. Take off the heat and let infuse for 20 minutes.

2. Pour the mixture through a very fine strainer into a clean saucepan, squeezing out the milk from the ground almonds.

3. Add the chocolate and stir over a low heat until the chocolate has melted. Serve immediately.

CHOCOLATE MILKSHAKE

MAKES 2 LARGE SHAKES

2½ cups milk
5 scoops chocolate ice cream
2 tablespoons drinking
chocolate powder
2 tablespoons ready-made
chocolate sauce (optional)

1. Place the milk, ice cream, and drinking chocolate in a food processor or blender and blend until thick and frothy.

2. Pour the liquid into two tall glasses. Stir in a tablespoon of your favorite chocolate sauce if using.

SUPER-RICH INDULGENT HOT CHOCOLATE

This is definitely a once-in-a-while treat-yourself drink. If you have a slightly sweeter tooth use a chocolate containing 50% cocoa solids.

MAKES 2 GENEROUS MUGS OR 4 SMALL TEACUPS

¾ cup whipping cream
1 vanilla bean, split down the center
4oz bittersweet chocolate
   (70% cocoa solids),
   broken into pieces
1⅔ cups full-fat milk
Whipped cream and grated
   chocolate, to serve

1. Pour the cream into a saucepan, add the split vanilla bean and slowly bring to a boil.

2. Take off the heat and add the broken-up chocolate. Stir until the chocolate has melted and the mixture is smooth then return to a low heat and stir in the milk. Heat through, then remove the vanilla bean.

3. Pour into mugs or teacups and top with a spoonful of whipped cream and a sprinkle of grated chocolate.

HOT MOCHALATTE

A classic combination of coffee and chocolate come together to make this creamy treat.

MAKES 2

2 tablespoons unsweetened cocoa powder
2 teaspoons instant coffee granules
1/4 cup superfine sugar
2 1/4 cups full-fat milk

1. Place the cocoa powder, coffee granules, and sugar in a small bowl and pour over 3–4 tablespoons boiling water. Mix to a smooth paste.
2. Heat the milk in a saucepan and whisk in the cocoa paste. Stir over a gentle heat until piping hot.

WHITE CHOCOLATE & STRAWBERRY SMOOTHIE

You could also use raspberries for this smoothie, but you may want to strain the seeds before serving.

MAKES 2

3 1/2oz white chocolate, broken into pieces
3/4 cup milk
9oz strawberries, washed and hulled

1. Put the chocolate and milk into a saucepan and stir over a gentle heat until the chocolate has melted. Let cool.
2. Place the strawberries and the cooled milk into a food processor or blender and blend until smooth. Pour into two glasses and serve the smoothies immediately.

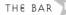

ICED CHOCOLATE

This recipe includes milk to make one iced chocolate, although there is enough chocolate syrup here for about ten drinks—but it will keep for at least a week in the fridge.

MAKES 1

1¾ cups water

1¼ cups granulated sugar

3½oz bittersweet chocolate (50–70% cocoa solids), broken into pieces

⅓ cup unsweetened cocoa powder, sieved

¾ cup cold milk

1. Place the water and sugar in a saucepan and heat slowly, stirring until the sugar has dissolved. Turn the heat up and boil for 5 minutes.

2. Take off the heat and stir in the chocolate and cocoa powder. Whisk until smooth. Let cool completely.

3. Pour about ¼ cup of the chocolate syrup (or to taste) into a large glass and add the cold milk. Stir well and top up with ice.

CHOCOLATE & MALTED MILK SMOOTHIE

Don't keep this childhood milkshake just for the kids—it's perfect as a wicked evening treat for adults too.

MAKES 2

1⅔ cups full-fat milk
¾ cup whipping cream
4 scoops chocolate ice cream, slightly softened
4 tablespoons Horlicks Drinking Powder

1. Place all the ingredients in a food processor or blender and blend until smooth. Serve chilled.

MILK CHOCOLATE & BANANA SMOOTHIE

This creamy smoothie is a bit like a drink version of a banana split—
wickedly indulgent. For an extra treat use full fat top milk.

MAKES 2

¾ cup milk
3½oz milk chocolate,
    broken into pieces
2 bananas
4 scoops vanilla ice cream

1. Bring the milk up to a boil, then take off the heat and whisk in the
chocolate. Let cool completely.

2. Pour the cooled chocolate milk into a food processor or blender and
add the remaining ingredients. Blend until smooth and frothy. Serve the
smoothies immediately.

VANILLA STRACCIATELLE SMOOTHIE

A delicious vanilla-flavored yogurt smoothie colored with specks of grated chocolate. It is a drinkable version of the Italian ice cream that has strands of chocolate running through it.

MAKES 2

2 cups vanilla-flavored yogurt or
    fromage frais
¾ cup cold milk
2oz milk chocolate, coarsely grated

1. Put the yogurt or fromage frais into a food processor or blender with the milk and blend until frothy.

2. Pour into a jug and stir in the grated chocolate. Serve immediately.

NEW WAYS WITH CHOCOLATE

ROAST PUMPKIN & CHOCOLATE SOUP

I like to roast the pumpkin as it seems to concentrate the flavor of the vegetable.

SERVES 4

3½lb pumpkin,
   seeds and rind removed
3 tablespoons olive oil
7oz red onions, peeled
   and finely chopped
2½ pints chicken stock
½oz bittersweet chocolate
   (99% cocoa solids), broken up
1 stick of cinnamon
Crème fraîche, to serve
Salt and freshly ground black pepper

1. Preheat the oven to 375°F. Cut the pumpkin flesh into 2in pieces, then spread the pieces onto a large baking sheet and spoon over 2 tablespoons of the olive oil. Season with salt and freshly ground black pepper and roast in the oven for 45 minutes.

2. Pour the remaining tablespoon of olive oil into a large saucepan and add the chopped onion. Cook over a low heat for 10–12 minutes until softened but not colored.

3. Add the roasted pumpkin to the pan and pour in the chicken stock. Add the chocolate and cinnamon stick. Bring to a boil, then turn the heat down and simmer for 20 minutes. Remove the cinnamon stick and let cool before liquidizing in a food processor or blender.

4. Taste the soup and season with plenty of salt and freshly ground black pepper. Serve each portion with a spoonful of crème fraîche and an extra sprinkling of freshly ground black pepper, if liked.

ROAST CHICKEN WITH BITTER CHOCOLATE GRAVY

Perfect with roast chicken, Bitter Chocolate Gravy is more of a jus than the thicker traditional gravy. It is quite a strong sauce, so a little goes a long way.

SERVES 4–5

1 lemon, cut into quarters
1 free-range chicken,
   weighing about 4lb
Half a head of garlic, separated
   into cloves, unpeeled
1 small bunch of fresh thyme
¾ stick (6 tablespoons) butter,
   slightly softened
2¼ cups chicken stock
1 tablespoon balsamic vinegar
1oz bitter chocolate
   (70% cocoa solids), broken up
Salt and freshly ground black pepper

1. Preheat the oven to 375°F. Stuff the lemon quarters into the chicken cavity along with the garlic cloves and half the thyme. Smear ½ stick (4 tablesoons) of the butter over the chicken and season with salt and freshly ground black pepper.

2. Place the chicken in a large roasting pan and cover with foil. Roast for 50 minutes, then remove the foil, baste, and continue to cook for 20–25 minutes. The chicken is done when the juices from the center of the leg run clear. Remove the chicken from the roasting pan, cover with foil, and let rest for 10–15 minutes.

3. Remove the leaves from the remaining thyme sprigs and chop finely. Pour off the fat from the roasting pan, leaving the juices and add the chopped thyme. Over a high heat add the chicken stock and balsamic vinegar and simmer for 5 minutes. Take off the heat, whisk in the chocolate, and stir until smooth.

4. Taste and season with salt and freshly ground black pepper. Whisk in the remaining ¼ stick (2 tablespoons) butter. Serve with the roast chicken.

TURKEY MOLE

You can just as well use cooked turkey in this recipe and in fact it is a great way of spicing up the remains of a Christmas turkey. Simply add the turkey after cooking the tomato sauce for 15 minutes and heat through.

SERVES 4

1 tablespoon vegetable oil
1 onion, peeled and finely sliced
2 sticks celery, finely chopped
2 green bell peppers, deseeded
   and finely chopped
2 garlic cloves, peeled
   and finely sliced
1 mild green chili, deseeded
   and finely chopped
1 small dried chili, crumbled
A couple of pinches of ground cumin
1½lb turkey breast or leg meat,
   cut into thin slices
13oz passata (strained
   chopped tomatoes)
½oz bittersweet chocolate
   (85% cocoa solids), broken up
Salt and freshly ground black pepper
TO SERVE
1 tablespoon toasted flaked almonds
2 tablespoons chopped fresh
   coriander

1. Heat the oil in a large skillet with a lid. Add the onion, celery, bell peppers, garlic, and green chili and cook over a low heat, stirring every now and again, for 15 minutes until the vegetables are soft.

2. Add the dried chili and pinches of cumin and stir in the sliced turkey. Cook for 5 minutes, stirring.

3. Pour in the passata and season with salt and freshly ground black pepper. Cover and simmer for 15–20 minutes. Stir in the chocolate and taste and season again if necessary.

4. Just before serving sprinkle over the flaked almonds and chopped fresh coriander.

CHILI CON CARNE

A touch of chocolate adds a velvety richness and a wonderful depth of flavor to the chili. I don't like it to be fiery hot, but if that is your preference you can up the quantity of dried chilies.

SERVES 4

1 tablespoon vegetable oil
9oz onions, peeled
  and finely chopped
3 garlic cloves, peeled and crushed
1³⁄₄lb beef mince
2 teaspoons ground cumin
1 teaspoon dried oregano
2 small dried hot chilies, crushed
2 tablespoons tomato purée
1 tablespoon tomato ketchup
1¼ cups beef or chicken stock
1 x 14oz can kidney beans,
  drained and rinsed
½oz bittersweet chocolate
  (99% cocoa solids), broken up
Salt and freshly ground black pepper
Sour cream, grated cheese, and
  tortilla chips, to serve

1. Heat the oil in a large saucepan, add the onions and garlic, and cook over a low heat for 10 minutes until softened.

2. Add the beef mince and turn the heat up. Stirring to break up the mince, brown for 3–4 minutes, then turn the heat down. Add the cumin, oregano, and crumbled chilies and cook for a further minute.

3. Stir in the tomato purée and tomato ketchup and then pour in the stock. Simmer the chilli con carne for 45 minutes.

4. Stir in the kidney beans and cook for a further 5 minutes. Stir in the chocolate and taste and season with salt and freshly ground black pepper.

5. Serve with sour cream, grated cheese, and tortilla chips on the side.

VENISON & CHOCOLATE CASSEROLE

This is the perfect dish for a cold winter's day—rich and warming. It is
preferable to marinate the venison overnight, but if you don't have the time
a couple of hours is better than nothing.

SERVES 4–5

2 cups red wine
2 garlic cloves, peeled and crushed
2 onions, peeled and finely sliced
2 bay leaves
2 sprigs of fresh rosemary
1 heaping teaspoon juniper berries,
    finely chopped
6 cloves
2 tablespoons olive oil
2 strips of orange peel
2lb shoulder or leg of venison,
    cut into 1½in pieces
3 large carrots, peeled
    and sliced into rounds
1¼ cups chicken or vegetable stock
¾oz bittersweet chocolate
    (85% cocoa solids), broken up
3 teaspoons cornstarch
Salt and freshly ground black pepper
Chopped fresh parsley, to garnish

1. Put the wine, garlic, onions, bay leaves, rosemary, juniper berries,
cloves, olive oil, and orange peel into a large bowl. Add the venison and
mix well. Cover and let marinate overnight.

2. Transfer to a casserole dish and add the carrots and stock. Slowly bring
to a boil and season with salt and freshly ground black pepper. Cover and
simmer for 2 hours by which time the meat should be very tender.

3. Stir in the chocolate and taste and season again if necessary. Mix
the cornstarch with 3 teaspoons cold water and stir into the casserole.
Heat through until thickened a little. Spoon onto serving dishes and
garnish with a sprinkling of chopped parsley.

ROAST RIB OF BEEF WITH CHOCOLATE & MADEIRA SAUCE

I think a rib of beef is the tastiest joint. It may not be as tender as a fillet, but the flavor wins hands down. Make sure the meat is at room temperature before roasting it, as it will affect the cooking time if it comes straight out of the refrigerator.

SERVES 4

1 tablespoon vegetable oil or dripping
1 onion, peeled and cut into eighths
1 carrot, peeled and roughly chopped
4 garlic cloves, unpeeled
4lb rib of beef, bone-in
1 tablespoon plain flour
⅓ cup Madeira
2 cups beef or chicken stock
½oz bittersweet chocolate
   (99% cocoa solids), broken up
Salt and freshly ground black pepper

1. Preheat the oven to 375°F. Pour the oil or dripping into a roasting pan and add the onion, carrot, and garlic cloves. Place the meat on top of the vegetables and season well with salt and freshly ground black pepper.

2. Roast for 60–80 minutes depending on how rare you like your meat. Lift out the beef, cover with foil, and let rest for 10–15 minutes.

3. Pour off all but a tablespoon of fat from the roasting pan, keeping the vegetables. Stir in the flour and cook over a low heat for a minute. Slowly whisk in the Madeira and cook for 3–4 minutes until thickened.

4. Add the stock and simmer, stirring, for a further 3–4 minutes. Add the chocolate and stir until melted. Taste and season if necessary.

5. Pass the sauce through a strainer squeezing out as much juice as you can from the vegetables.

6. Carve the meat and serve the sauce separately.

ROAST PHEASANT WITH SALSA AGRODOLCE

A salsa agrodolce is a sweet-sour sauce that here is enriched with a touch of bittersweet chocolate.

SERVES 6

3 small hen pheasants
½ stick (4 tablespoons) butter, softened
Small bunch of fresh thyme
Salt and freshly ground black pepper
2 tablespoons chopped fresh thyme, to serve

FOR THE SALSA AGRODOLCE

1 tablespoon butter
1 onion, peeled and finely chopped
2 tablespoons superfine sugar
3 tablespoons red wine vinegar
¾ cup red wine
⅔ cup chicken stock
½oz bittersweet chocolate (80% cocoa solids), broken up
¼ stick (2 tablespoons) sweet butter

1. Preheat the oven to 375°F. Place the pheasants in a large roasting pan and rub over the butter. Stuff each cavity with the thyme sprigs and season well with salt and freshly ground black pepper. Roast for about 50–55 minutes or until a skewer inserted into the leg joint feels piping hot. Remove from the oven, cover, and let rest for 10 minutes.

2. While the pheasants are roasting you can make the salsa agrodolce. Melt the butter in a small saucepan and add the onion. Cook slowly for 10 minutes until the onions are softened but not colored. Spoon into a bowl and set aside.

3. In the same pan add the superfine sugar and red wine vinegar. Over a gentle heat stir until the sugar has dissolved, then turn the heat up and boil until the liquid has reduced to almost nothing. Pour in the wine and stock, add the reserved onions, and simmer for 15 minutes. Take off the heat and whisk in the chocolate followed by the sweet butter. Taste the sauce and season with salt and plenty of freshly ground black pepper.

4. Serve slices of the pheasant with a little sauce and chopped thyme scattered over to finish.

CHORIZO, WHITE BEAN & CHOCOLATE RAGOÛT

A great time-saving alternative is to use three 14oz cans of drained cannellini beans in place of the dried beans—simply add them at step 4.

SERVES 4

11oz dried cannellini beans
½ onion, peeled
1 stick of celery
5 sprigs of fresh thyme
1 bay leaf

FOR THE RAGOÛT

3 tablespoons olive oil
2 medium-sized onions, peeled and
    finely chopped
1 carrot, peeled and finely diced
2 cloves garlic, finely chopped
14oz can chopped tomatoes
1 cup red wine
1⅔ cups chicken stock or water
1 tablespoon chopped fresh rosemary,
    plus 4 extra sprigs, to serve
11oz chorizo sausage, skin removed
    and sliced into ¼in discs
½oz bittersweet chocolate
    (99% cocoa solids), broken up
Salt and freshly ground black pepper

1. Put the dried beans into a large bowl and fill with cold water. Let soak overnight.

2. Drain the beans and put in a large saucepan with the onion, celery, thyme, and bay leaf. Fill the saucepan two-thirds full with cold water. Bring to a boil, then turn the heat down and simmer for 45–50 minutes or until the beans are soft. Drain and set aside.

3. To make the ragoût, wipe out the pan and add the olive oil, chopped onions, carrot, and garlic. Cook over a low heat for 10 minutes until the vegetables have softened but not colored. Add the chopped tomatoes, wine, stock or water, and chopped rosemary. Bring to a boil, then turn the heat down and simmer for 10 minutes.

4. Add the cooked beans and chorizo and cook for a further 15 minutes. Take off the heat and stir in the chocolate.

5. Taste the ragoût and season with salt and freshly ground black pepper. Spoon into four serving bowls and garnish each with a sprig of rosemary.

BAKED HAM WITH CHOCOLATE GLAZE

This is an interesting and delicious alternative to the traditional honey and mustard glaze for ham. I prefer this version served cold with a crunchy salad and baked potato.

SERVES 6

6lb piece of unsmoked gammon,
   bone-in
1 onion
1 stick of celery
1 carrot, peeled and halved
1 teaspoon whole cloves
FOR THE GLAZE
²⁄₃ cup light brown sugar
¹⁄₃ cup cider vinegar
¹⁄₄ cup ginger wine
1¹⁄₂oz bittersweet chocolate
   (70% cocoa solids), broken up
Pinch of ground cloves
Salt and freshly ground black pepper

1. Put the gammon into a large saucepan and cover with water. Bring to a boil and then remove from the heat and drain.

2. Cover with cold water and add the onion, celery, carrot, and cloves. Bring to aa boil, then turn the heat down and simmer for 2 hours.

3. Meanwhile, make the glaze. Put the sugar, vinegar, and ginger wine into a saucepan and slowly bring to a boil. Simmer for 5 minutes.

4. Take off the heat and whisk in the chocolate. Season with a little salt and freshly ground black pepper and stir in the ground cloves.

5. Preheat the oven to 375°F. Drain the gammon and put it in a large roasting pan.

6. Pour the chocolate glaze over the gammon. Roast in the oven for 20 minutes, basting the joint every 5 minutes with the chocolate glaze. Remove from the oven and let rest for 10–15 minutes before serving.

CHOCOLATE & PEPPERED STEAK

Try and find some flavorsome, well-hung meats for this dish. Fillet steak may be the most tender, but it is often lacking in flavor.

SERVES 2

2 x 7oz sirloin steaks
   at room temperature
1 teaspoon sunflower oil
1 tablespoon crushed black
   peppercorns
¼oz bittersweet chocolate
   (99% cocoa solids), grated
Salt

1. Put the steaks onto a plate and brush with the oil. Press the peppercorns evenly over both sides and season with salt.

2. Heat a skillet until hot and fry the steaks for 1–2 minutes each side, depending on their thickness and how well-done you like them.

3. Remove the steaks to serving plates and sprinkle over the chocolate. Let rest for a couple of minutes, then serve.

TIP
Never be afraid to let any meat, red or white, rest. It allows it to relax as the juices disperse, and this helps the meat to retain its moisture.

CHOCOLATE, TOMATO & CHILI PASTA

SERVES 4

14oz 00 flour (available
   in most supermarkets)
$1/3$oz cocoa powder
4 eggs
Grated parmesan, to serve
FOR THE TOMATO CHILI SAUCE
2 tablespoons olive oil
2 garlic cloves, peeled
   and finely chopped
1 tablespoon rosemary leaves,
   finely chopped
2 x 14oz cans chopped tomatoes
1 dried chili, crumbled
Pinch of superfine sugar
Small bunch of fresh basil,
   roughly torn
Salt and freshly ground black pepper

1. Put the flour and cocoa powder into a food processor and process for a few seconds until mixed together. Add the eggs and process until the mixture has formed into rough breadcrumbs.

2. Tip out onto a lightly floured work surface and knead just until the dough is smooth. Divide into four pieces. Start on the widest setting on the pasta machine and feed the dough through the rollers. Dust the strip of dough with flour.

3. Narrow the setting and feed the dough through again. Keep doing this, dusting with flour each time, until you have finished on the narrowest setting. Once you have a long strip of pasta dough, dust with flour and fold four or five times over, then cut into $1/4$in strips. Repeat for the remaining three pieces of dough.

4. To make the sauce, heat the olive oil in a saucepan and add the garlic and rosemary. Cook for a minute, then pour in the chopped tomatoes and chili. Season with salt and freshly ground black pepper and add a pinch of sugar. Cook for 30–40 minutes until the sauce is really thick. Just before serving stir in the torn basil leaves.

5. Meanwhile, cook the pasta in a large pan of salted boiling water for 3–4 minutes. Drain and toss with the tomato sauce. Serve fresh grated Parmesan on the side.

INDEX